Math in Focus®
Singapore Math
by Marshall Cavendish

Workbook

Consultant and Author
Dr. Fong Ho Kheong

Authors
Chelvi Ramakrishnan and Gan Kee Soon

U.S. Consultants
Dr. Richard Bisk, Andy Clark, and Patsy F. Kanter

Marshall Cavendish
Education

U.S. Distributor

Houghton
Mifflin
Harcourt

© 2015 Marshall Cavendish International (Singapore) Private Limited

Published by Marshall Cavendish Education
An imprint of Marshall Cavendish International (Singapore) Private Limited
Times Centre, 1 New Industrial Road, Singapore 536196
Customer Service Hotline: (65) 6411 0820
E-mail: tmesales@sg.marshallcavendish.com
Website: www.marshallcavendish.com/education

Distributed by
Houghton Mifflin Harcourt
222 Berkeley Street
Boston, MA 02116
Tel: 617-351-5000
Website: www.hmheducation.com/mathinfocus

First published 2015

Math in Focus® Workbook 5B
ISBN 978-0-544-19389-5

Printed in Singapore

1 2 3 4 5 6 7 8 1401   20 19 18 17 16 15
4500421125   A B C D E

Contents

Decimals

Multiplying and Dividing Decimals

10 Percent

11 Graphs and Probability

12 Angles

13 Properties of Triangles and Four-Sided Figures

14 Surface Area and Volume

Decimals

Practice 1   Understanding Thousandths

Write the decimal shown in each place-value chart.

Example

Ones		Tenths	Hundredths	Thousandths
		○ ○	○ ○ ○	○ ○ ○ ○ ○ ○ ○

__0.237__

1.

Ones		Tenths	Hundredths	Thousandths
○ ○ ○ ○			○ ○ ○ ○ ○	○ ○ ○ ○ ○

__4. 0 5 5__

2.

Ones		Tenths	Hundredths	Thousandths
○ ○ ○ ○ ○ ○				○ ○ ○ ○ ○ ○ ○ ○ ○

__4.009__

Write the decimal shown in the place-value chart.

3.

Ones	Tenths	Hundredths	Thousandths
○ ○ ○ ○ ○	○ ○	○	

5.210

Mark X to show where each decimal is located.

4.   0.006   5.   0.024   6.   0.033

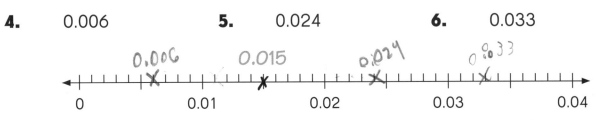

Write the decimal shown by each arrow.

7.

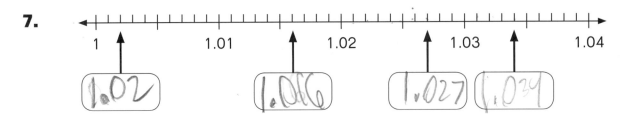

1.02   1.066   1.027   1.024

Complete.

.04
8.   4 hundredths = _____ thousandths

.85
9.   8 tenths 5 hundredths = _____ thousandths

.020
10.   20 thousandths = _____ hundredths

.125
11.   125 thousandths = 1 tenth _____ thousandths

Complete.

12.   0.126 = 1 tenth 2 hundredths _____ thousandths

13.   0.352 = 3 tenths _____ hundredths 2 thousandths

Write the equivalent decimal.

14.   7 thousandths = _____   **15.**   19 thousandths = _____

16.   235 thousandths = _____   **17.**   300 thousandths = _____

Write each fraction as a decimal.

18. $\dfrac{13}{1000}$ = _____   **19.** $\dfrac{55}{1000}$ = _____

20. $\dfrac{228}{1000}$ = _____   **21.** $\dfrac{430}{1000}$ = _____

Write each mixed number as a decimal.

22. $2\dfrac{3}{1000}$ = _____   **23.** $6\dfrac{61}{1000}$ = _____

24. $7\dfrac{107}{1000}$ = _____   **25.** $8\dfrac{240}{1000}$ = _____

Write each improper fraction as a decimal.

26. $\dfrac{1005}{1000}$ = _____   **27.** $\dfrac{1013}{1000}$ = _____

28. $\dfrac{2341}{1000}$ = _____   **29.** $\dfrac{3450}{1000}$ = _____

Complete.

30. 0.014 = _____ thousandths

31. 0.178 = _____ thousandths

32. 0.76 = _____ thousandths

33. 1.035 = 1 one and _____ thousandths

**1.234 can be written in expanded form as $1 + \dfrac{2}{10} + \dfrac{3}{100} + \dfrac{4}{1000}$.
Write each decimal in expanded notation.**

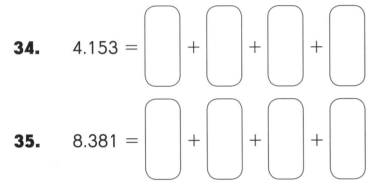

34. 4.153 = ⬭ + ⬭ + ⬭ + ⬭

35. 8.381 = ⬭ + ⬭ + ⬭ + ⬭

**9.876 can be written in expanded form as $9 + 0.8 + 0.07 + 0.006$.
Write each decimal in expanded notation.**

36. 6.426 = _____ + _____ + _____ + _____

37. 3.642 = _____ + _____ + _____ + _____

Complete.

In 5.074,

38. the digit 4 is in the _____ place.

39. the value of the digit 7 is _____.

40. the digit 0 is in the _____ place.

41. the digit 5 stands for _____.

Practice 2   Comparing and Rounding Decimals

Compare the decimals in each place-value chart.

Fill in the blanks. Write > or < in the ◯.

Example

Ones	Tenths	Hundredths	Thousandths
0	0	2	
0	0	1	5

__0.02__ is greater than __0.015__.

__0.02__ (>) __0.015__

1.

Ones	Tenths	Hundredths	Thousandths
0	3	0	8
0	2	9	

_____ is less than _____.

_____ ◯ _____

2.

Ones	Tenths	Hundredths	Thousandths
4	0	9	1
4	1	9	

_____ is less than _____.

_____ ◯ _____

Write the greater decimal.

3.   11.6 or 21.8 _____

4.   10.55 or 10.05 _____

5.   20.07 or 20.01 _____

6.   100.202 or 100.212 _____

Write >, <, or = in each ( ).

7.   3.7 ( ) 0.370   **8.**   0.150 ( ) 0.51

9.   0.205 ( ) 2.05   **10.**   2.3 ( ) 2.30

Circle the greatest decimal and underline the least.

11.   1.03,   1.3,   0.13   **12.**   0.5,   0.53,   0.503

13.   2.35,   2.305,   2.035   **14.**   8.7,   8.07,   8.701

Order the decimals from least to greatest.

> *Example*
>
> 3.33,   3.03,   3.303   3.03,   3.303,   3.33

15.   5.51,   5.051,   5.501   _____

16.   4,   4.01,   4.001   _____

17.   0.023,   0.203,   0.230   _____

Write the missing decimal in each box. Round the given decimal to the nearest hundredth.

18.

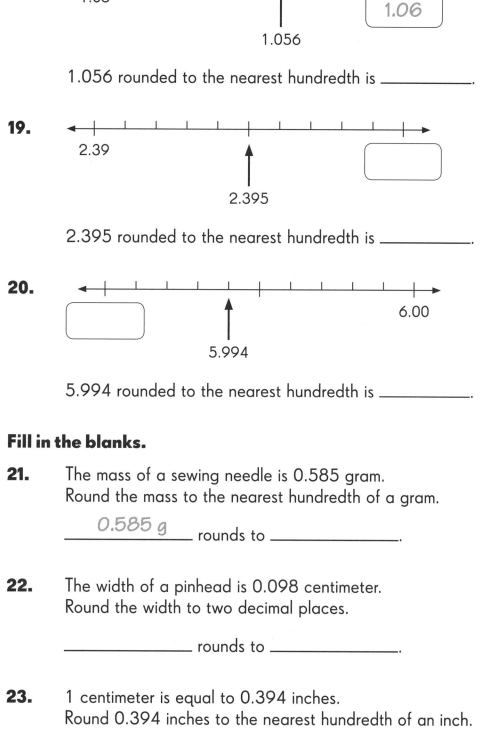

1.056 rounded to the nearest hundredth is _____.

19.

2.395 rounded to the nearest hundredth is _____.

20.

5.994 rounded to the nearest hundredth is _____.

Fill in the blanks.

21. The mass of a sewing needle is 0.585 gram.
Round the mass to the nearest hundredth of a gram.

_____0.585 g_____ rounds to _____.

22. The width of a pinhead is 0.098 centimeter.
Round the width to two decimal places.

_____ rounds to _____.

23. 1 centimeter is equal to 0.394 inches.
Round 0.394 inches to the nearest hundredth of an inch.

_____ rounds to _____.

Round each decimal to the nearest whole number, nearest tenth, and nearest hundredth.

24.

Decimal	Rounded to the Nearest		
	Whole Number	**Tenth**	**Hundredth**
1.049			
3.753			
2.199			

Fill in the blanks.

25.   A decimal rounded to the nearest tenth is 2.5.
Write two decimals that can be rounded to 2.5.

_____ and _____

26.   A decimal rounded to the nearest hundredth is 4.09.
Write two decimals that can be rounded to 4.09.

_____ and _____

27.   A decimal rounded to the nearest hundredth is 6.32.
This decimal is greater than 6.32.

What could this decimal be? _____

28.   A decimal rounded to the nearest hundredth is 7.01.
This decimal is less than 7.01.

What could this decimal be? _____

Practice 3   Rewriting Decimals as Fractions and Mixed Numbers

Rewrite each decimal as a fraction or mixed number in simplest form.

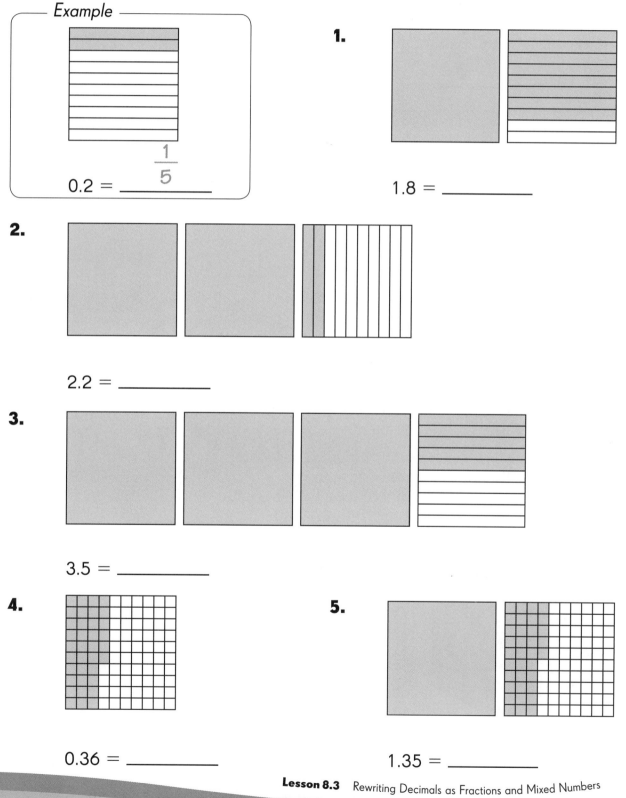

Example

$0.2 =$ _____ $\dfrac{1}{5}$

1.

$1.8 =$ _____

2.

$2.2 =$ _____

3.

$3.5 =$ _____

4.

$0.36 =$ _____

5.

$1.35 =$ _____

Rewrite each decimal as a fraction or mixed number in simplest form.

6.

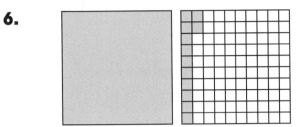

1.12 = _____

7.

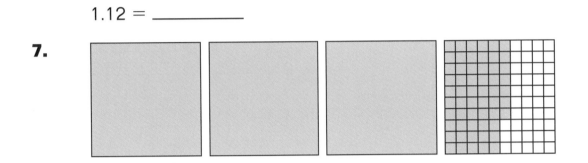

3.57 = _____

8.

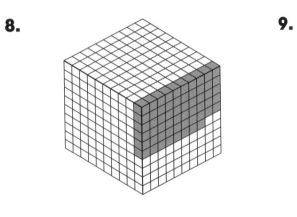

0.058 = _____

9.

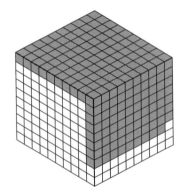

0.169 = _____

10.

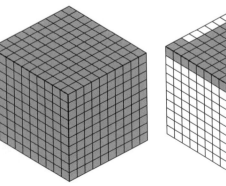

1.092 = _____

Rewrite the decimal as a mixed number in simplest form.

11.

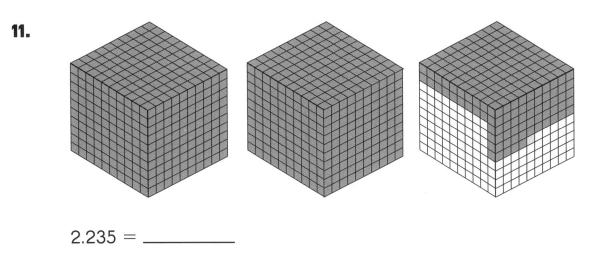

2.235 = _____

Rewrite each decimal as a fraction or mixed number in simplest form.

12. 7.3

13. 26.9

14. 0.59

15. 15.82

16. 1.28

17. 4.109

18. 0.136

19. 3.602

Math Journal

1. Explain why 1.8, 1.80, and 1.800 have the same value.

2. Howard does not know how to find the values of A and B on the number line. Write the steps Howard should use to find these values.

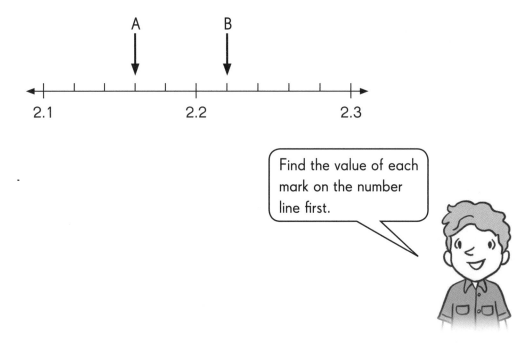

Find the value of each mark on the number line first.

Put On Your Thinking Cap!

Challenging Practice

Solve.

1. You are given two numbers, 3.987 and 70.140.

    a. Round each number to the nearest tenth.

    b. Round each number to the nearest hundredth.

    c. Find the difference between your rounded answers for 3.987.

    d Find the difference between your rounded answers for 70.140.

    e. Are your answers in Exercises **a** and **b** the same? Explain why or why not.

Complete.

2. $4.129 = 4 + \dfrac{1}{10} + \dfrac{29}{\boxed{}}$

3. $2.075 = 2 + \dfrac{\boxed{}}{1000} + \dfrac{5}{\boxed{}}$

4. $3.157 = \dfrac{\boxed{}}{1000} + \dfrac{7}{1000}$

Put On Your Thinking Cap!

Problem Solving

Solve. Show your work.

1. Kimberly has 3.25 kilograms of flour in a container. She adds 45 grams of flour to the container. How many kilograms of flour does she have now?

2. The weight of four objects are $3\frac{1}{5}$ pounds, $3\frac{39}{1000}$ pounds, $3\frac{99}{100}$ pounds, and $3\frac{52}{10}$ pounds. Arrange the weights in order from least to greatest.

Chapter 9 Multiplying and Dividing Decimals

Practice 1   Multiplying Decimals

Multiply. Write the product as a decimal.

Example

$2 \times 0.3 = 2 \times$ _____3_____ tenths

$\quad\quad\quad\quad = $ _____6_____ tenths

$\quad\quad\quad\quad = $ _____0.6_____

So, $2 \times 0.3 = $ _____0.6_____.

1. $5 \times 0.6 = 5 \times$ _____ tenths

$\quad\quad\quad\quad = $ _____ tenths

$\quad\quad\quad\quad = $ _____ or _____

So, $5 \times 0.6 = $ _____.

2. $7 \times 0.8 = 7 \times$ _____ tenths

$\quad\quad\quad\quad = $ _____ tenths

$\quad\quad\quad\quad = $ _____

So, $7 \times 0.8 = $ _____.

3. $10 \times 0.4 = 10 \times$ _____ tenths

$\quad\quad\quad\quad = $ _____ tenths

$\quad\quad\quad\quad = $ _____ or _____

So, $10 \times 0.4 = $ _____.

Multiply. Write the product as a decimal.

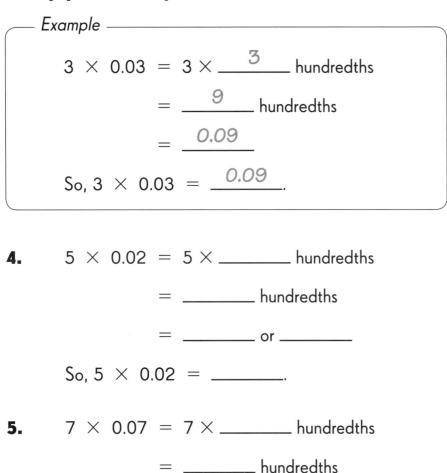

— Example —

$3 \times 0.03 = 3 \times$ _____3_____ hundredths

$ =$ _____9_____ hundredths

$ =$ _____0.09_____

So, $3 \times 0.03 =$ _____0.09_____.

---

4. $5 \times 0.02 = 5 \times$ _____ hundredths

$ =$ _____ hundredths

$ =$ _____ or _____

So, $5 \times 0.02 =$ _____.

5. $7 \times 0.07 = 7 \times$ _____ hundredths

$ =$ _____ hundredths

$ =$ _____

So, $7 \times 0.07 =$ _____.

6. $6 \times 0.12 = 6 \times$ _____ hundredths

$ =$ _____ hundredths

$ =$ _____

So, $6 \times 0.12 =$ _____.

Follow the steps to multiply 2.6 by 3. Fill in the blanks.

7. Step 1

```
   2 . 6
×      3
─────────
```

Multiply the tenths by 3.

3 × 6 tenths = _____ tenths

Regroup the tenths.

_____ tenths = _____ one and _____ tenths

Step 2

```
   2 . 6
×      3
─────────
```

Multiply the ones by 3.

3 × 2 ones = _____ ones

Add the ones.

_____ ones + _____ one = _____ ones

So, 3 × 2.6 = _____.

Multiply.

8.
```
   0 . 3
×      8
─────────
```

9.
```
   2 . 6
×      4
─────────
```

10.
```
   7 . 9
×      5
─────────
```

11.
```
  1 2 . 4
×        7
─────────
```

Follow the steps to multiply 1.46 by 6. Fill in the blanks.

12.   Step 1

$$\begin{array}{r} 1.46 \\ \times6 \\ \hline \end{array}$$

Multiply the hundredths by 6.

6 × 6 hundredths = _____ hundredths

Regroup the hundredths.

_____ hundredths = _____ tenths _____ hundredths

Step 2

$$\begin{array}{r} 1.46 \\ \times6 \\ \hline \end{array}$$

Multiply the tenths by 6.

6 × 4 tenths = _____ tenths

Add the tenths.

_____ tenths + _____ tenths = _____ tenths

Regroup the tenths.

_____ tenths = _____ ones and _____ tenths

Step 3

$$\begin{array}{r} 1.46 \\ \times6 \\ \hline \end{array}$$

Multiply the ones by 6.

6 × 1 one = _____ ones

Add the ones.

_____ ones + _____ ones = _____ ones

So, 6 × 1.46 = _____.

Multiply.

13.
$$\begin{array}{r} 1\,0\,.\,0\,7 \\ \times \qquad 5 \\ \hline \end{array}$$

14.
$$\begin{array}{r} 0\,.\,7\,5 \\ \times \qquad 4 \\ \hline \end{array}$$

15.
$$\begin{array}{r} 3\,.\,0\,6 \\ \times \qquad 9 \\ \hline \end{array}$$

16.
$$\begin{array}{r} 1\,5\,.\,2\,4 \\ \times \qquad 8 \\ \hline \end{array}$$

17. $4 \times 2.08 = $ _____

18. $3 \times 3.29 = $ _____

19. $7 \times 5.71 = $ _____

20. $6 \times 4.81 = $ _____

21. $9 \times 7.46 = $ _____

22. $8 \times 6.52 = $ _____

Write the correct decimal in each box.

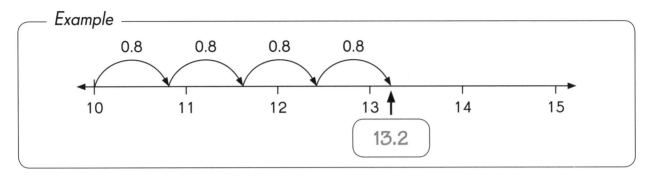

Example

0.8   0.8   0.8   0.8

10   11   12   13   14   15

13.2

23.

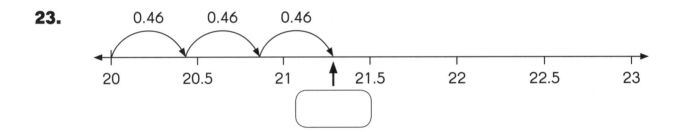

0.46   0.46   0.46

20   20.5   21   21.5   22   22.5   23

24.

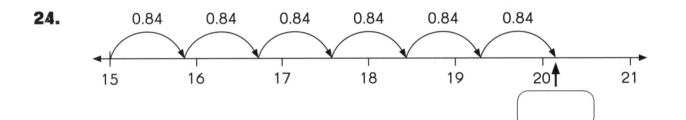

0.84   0.84   0.84   0.84   0.84   0.84

15   16   17   18   19   20   21

25.

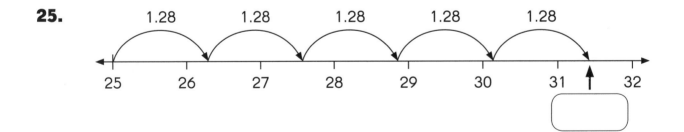

1.28   1.28   1.28   1.28   1.28

25   26   27   28   29   30   31   32

Name: _____ Date: _____

Practice 2   Multiplying by Tens, Hundreds, or Thousands

Complete. Draw chips and use arrows to show how the chips move. Then fill in the blanks.

1.

	Hundreds	Tens	Ones	Tenths	Hundredths
12		○	○ ○		
12 × 10	○	○ ○			

2			○ ○		
2 × 10					

0.2				○ ○	
0.2 × 10					

0.12				○	○ ○
0.12 × 10					

$12 \times 10 = $ _____ $2 \times 10 = $ _____

$0.2 \times 10 = $ _____ $0.12 \times 10 = $ _____

Multiply.

2. $0.5 \times 10 = $ _____   **3.** $1.9 \times 10 = $ _____

4. $3.42 \times 10 = $ _____   **5.** $7.035 \times 10 = $ _____

6. $10 \times 7.9 = $ _____   **7.** $10 \times 4.8 = $ _____

8. $10 \times 27.54 = $ _____   **9.** $10 \times 12.009 = $ _____

Complete.

10. $0.7 \times$ _____ $= 7$

11. $15.72 \times$ _____ $= 157.2$

12. $10 \times$ _____ $= 534.2$

13. _____ $\times 10 = 19.07$

Complete.

─ *Example* ───────────────

$8 \times 50 = (8 \times \underline{\quad 5 \quad}) \times 10$

$\qquad\qquad = \underline{\quad 40 \quad} \times 10$

$\qquad\qquad = \underline{\quad 400 \quad}$

So, $8 \times 50 = \underline{\quad 400 \quad}$.

──────────────────────────

14. $0.8 \times 50 = (0.8 \times 5) \times$ _____

$\qquad\qquad\quad = $ _____ $\times 10$

$\qquad\qquad\quad = $ _____

So, $0.8 \times 50 = $ _____.

15. $0.88 \times 50 = (0.88 \times$ _____ $) \times 10$

$\qquad\qquad\quad\; = $ _____ $\times 10$

$\qquad\qquad\quad\; = $ _____

So, $0.88 \times 50 = $ _____.

Find each product.

16. $0.9 \times 40 = $ _____

17. $1.5 \times 60 = $ _____

18. $0.05 \times 80 = $ _____

19. $9.17 \times 70 = $ _____

20. $6.358 \times 30 = $ _____

21. $34.6 \times 50 = $ _____

22. $41.32 \times 60 = $ _____

23. $23.05 \times 40 = $ _____

Multiply.

24. 1.3 × 100 = _____

25. 6.8 × 100 = _____

26. 4.196 × 100 = _____

27. 100 × 74.3 = _____

28. 46.8 × 100 = _____

29. 4.68 × 100 = _____

30. 5.095 × 100 = _____

31. 100 × 50.95 = _____

Multiply.

32. 1.8 × 1,000 = _____

33. 2.1 × 1,000 = _____

34. 9.097 × 1,000 = _____

35. 1,000 × 7.007 = _____

36. 2.74 × 1,000 = _____

37. 27.4 × 1,000 = _____

38. 1,000 × 10.81 = _____

39. 108.1 × 1,000 = _____

Complete.

Example

1.2 = 0.12 × ___10___

= 0.012 × ___100___

40. 360 = 36 × _____

= 3.6 × _____

= 0.36 × _____

41. 438 = _____ × 10

= _____ × 100

= _____ × 1,000

42. 7,256 = _____ × 10

= _____ × 100

= _____ × 1,000

Complete.

43. $0.8 \times 10^2 = 0.8 \times (\underline{} \times 10)$

$= 0.8 \times \underline{}$

$= \underline{}$

44. $0.96 \times 10^2 = 0.96 \times (\underline{} \times 10)$

$= 0.96 \times \underline{}$

$= \underline{}$

45. $0.065 \times 10^2 = 0.065 \times (\underline{} \times 10)$

$= 0.065 \times \underline{}$

$= \underline{}$

46. $13.8 \times 10^2 = 13.8 \times (\underline{} \times \underline{})$

$= 13.8 \times \underline{}$

$= \underline{}$

47. $9.849 \times 10^2 = 9.849 \times (\underline{} \times \underline{})$

$= 9.849 \times \underline{}$

$= \underline{}$

48. $0.2 \times 10^3 = 0.2 \times ($ _____ $\times 10 \times 10)$

   $= 0.2 \times$ _____

   $=$ _____

49. $0.06 \times 10^3 = 0.06 \times ($ _____ $\times$ _____ $\times 10)$

   $= 0.06 \times$ _____

   $=$ _____

50. $12.7 \times 10^3 = 12.7 \times ($ _____ $\times$ _____ $\times 10)$

   $= 12.7 \times$ _____

   $=$ _____

51. $2.007 \times 10^3 = 2.007 \times ($ _____ $\times$ _____ $\times$ _____ $)$

   $= 2.007 \times$ _____

   $=$ _____

Write 10, 10^2, or 10^3.

52. $12.2 \times$ _____ $= 1{,}220$

53. $0.7 \times$ _____ $= 700$

54. $1.5 \times$ _____ $= 150$

55. $181.8 \times$ _____ $= 1{,}818$

Multiply.

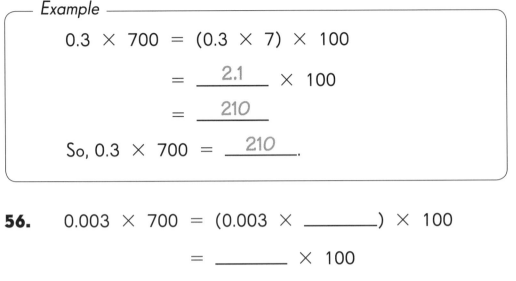

Example

$$0.3 \times 700 = (0.3 \times 7) \times 100$$

$$= \underline{2.1} \times 100$$

$$= \underline{210}$$

So, $0.3 \times 700 = \underline{210}$.

56. $0.003 \times 700 = (0.003 \times \underline{}) \times 100$

$$= \underline{} \times 100$$

$$= \underline{}$$

So, $0.003 \times 700 = \underline{}$.

57. $0.03 \times 2,000 = (0.03 \times \underline{}) \times 1,000$

$$= \underline{} \times 1,000$$

$$= \underline{}$$

So, $0.03 \times 2,000 = \underline{}$.

58. $0.003 \times 2,000 = (0.003 \times \underline{}) \times 1,000$

$$= \underline{} \times 1,000$$

$$= \underline{}$$

So, $0.003 \times 2,000 = \underline{}$.

Find each product.

59. $0.49 \times 300 = \underline{}$ **60.** $3.148 \times 500 = \underline{}$

61. $900 \times 3.18 = \underline{}$ **62.** $1.8 \times 2,000 = \underline{}$

63. $4,000 \times 2.5 = \underline{}$ **64.** $72.5 \times 6,000 = \underline{}$

Practice 3   Dividing Decimals

Divide. Write the quotient as a decimal.

― *Example* ―――――――――――――――――

$0.6 \div 2 =$ ___6___ tenths $\div 2$

$\qquad = $ ___3___ tenths

$\qquad = $ ___0.3___

So, $0.6 \div 2 =$ ___0.3___.

---

1. $\quad 0.8 \div 4 =$ _____ tenths $\div 4$

$\qquad\qquad = $ _____ tenths

$\qquad\qquad = $ _____

So, $0.8 \div 4 =$ _____.

2. $\quad 1 \div 5 =$ _____ tenths $\div 5$

$\qquad\qquad = $ _____ tenths

$\qquad\qquad = $ _____

So, $1 \div 5 =$ _____.

3. $\quad 2.4 \div 6 =$ _____ tenths $\div 6$

$\qquad\qquad = $ _____ tenths

$\qquad\qquad = $ _____

So, $2.4 \div 6 =$ _____.

Complete. Write the quotient as a decimal.

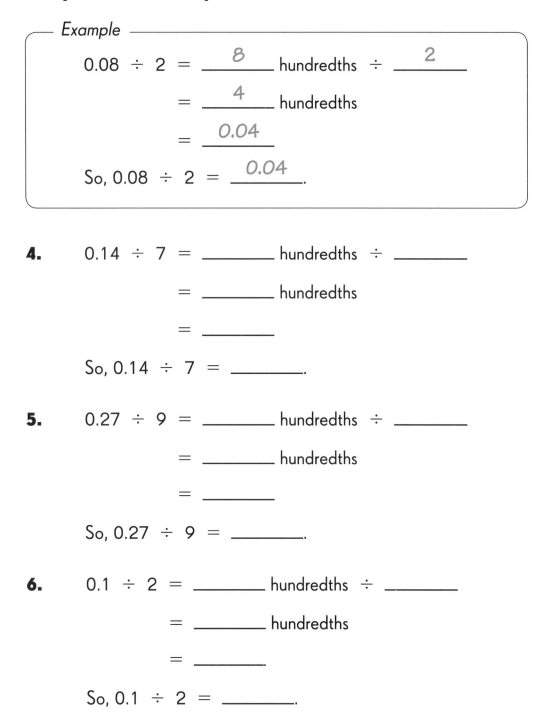

> *Example*
>
> 0.08 ÷ 2 = _____8_____ hundredths ÷ _____2_____
>
> = _____4_____ hundredths
>
> = _0.04_
>
> So, 0.08 ÷ 2 = _0.04_.

4.   0.14 ÷ 7 = _____ hundredths ÷ _____

= _____ hundredths

= _____

So, 0.14 ÷ 7 = _____.

5.   0.27 ÷ 9 = _____ hundredths ÷ _____

= _____ hundredths

= _____

So, 0.27 ÷ 9 = _____.

6.   0.1 ÷ 2 = _____ hundredths ÷ _____

= _____ hundredths

= _____

So, 0.1 ÷ 2 = _____.

Follow the steps to divide 8.4 by 3. Fill in the blanks.

7.   Step 1

3⟌8.4   Divide the ones by 3.

8 ones ÷ 3 = _____ ones R _____ ones

3⟌8.4   Regroup the remainder into tenths.

_____ ones = _____ tenths

Add the tenths.

_____ tenths + 4 tenths = _____ tenths

Step 2

3⟌8.4   Divide the tenths by 3.

_____ tenths ÷ 3 = _____ tenths

So, 8.4 ÷ 3 = _____ .

Divide.

8.   3)12.9

9.   8)5.6

10.   3)8.7

11.   9)24.3

12.   4)0.6

13.   5)5.2

Follow the steps to divide 5.48 by 4. Fill in the blanks.

14.   Step 1

4)5 . 4 8   Divide the ones by 4.

5 ones ÷ 4 = _____ one R _____ one

Regroup the remainder into tenths.

_____ one = _____ tenths

Add the tenths.

_____ tenths + 4 tenths = _____ tenths

Step 2

4)5 . 4 8   Divide the tenths by 4.

_____ tenths ÷ 4 = _____ tenths R _____ tenths

Regroup the remainder into hundredths.

_____ tenths = _____ hundredths

Add the hundredths.

_____ hundredths + 8 hundredths = _____ hundredths

Step 3

4) 5 . 4 8   Divide the hundredths by 4.

_____ hundredths ÷ 4 = _____ hundredths

So, 5.48 ÷ 4 = _____.

Divide.

15. $4\overline{)0.52}$

16. $9\overline{)0.81}$

17. $6\overline{)12.12}$

18. $7\overline{)9.66}$

19. $5\overline{)15.65}$

20. $4\overline{)3}$

Name: _____   **Date:** _____

Divide. Round each quotient to the nearest tenth.

Example

$7 \div 8$

$$
\begin{array}{r}
0.87 \\
8{\overline{\smash{)}\,7.00}} \\
\underline{0} \\
7\ 0 \\
\underline{6\ 4} \\
6\ 0 \\
\underline{5\ 6} \\
4
\end{array}
$$

$7 \div 8$ is about 0.9.

First, divide to two decimal places. Then round the answer to the nearest tenth.

21. $5 \div 7$

$7{\overline{\smash{)}\,5}}$

22. $11 \div 9$

$9{\overline{\smash{)}\,1\ \ 1}}$

Divide. Round each quotient to the nearest hundredth.

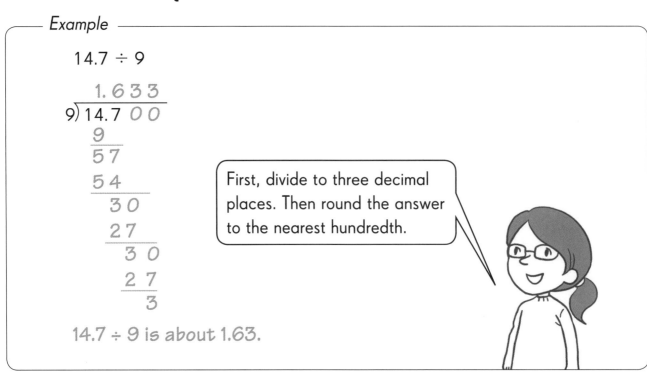

Example

14.7 ÷ 9

```
      1. 6 3 3
9) 14.7 0 0
    9
    5 7
    5 4
      3 0
      2 7
        3 0
        2 7
          3
```

First, divide to three decimal places. Then round the answer to the nearest hundredth.

14.7 ÷ 9 is about 1.63.

23.   3.2 ÷ 7

```
7) 3 . 2
```

24.   13 ÷ 6

```
6) 1   3
```

Practice 4   Dividing by Tens, Hundreds, or Thousands

Complete. Draw chips and use arrows to show how the chips move. Then fill in the blanks.

1.

	Hundreds	Tens	Ones	Tenths	Hundredths
140	○	○○○○			
140 ÷ 10		○	○○○○		

	Hundreds	Tens	Ones	Tenths	Hundredths
20		○○			
20 ÷ 10					

	Hundreds	Tens	Ones	Tenths	Hundredths
6			○○○ ○○○		
6 ÷ 10					

	Hundreds	Tens	Ones	Tenths	Hundredths
0.3				○○○	
0.3 ÷ 10					

$140 \div 10 = $ _____ $20 \div 10 = $ _____

$6 \div 10 = $ _____ $0.3 \div 10 = $ _____

Divide.

2. $6 \div 10 = $ _____   **3.** $54 \div 10 = $ _____

4. $215 \div 10 = $ _____   **5.** $5.2 \div 10 = $ _____

6. $64.6 \div 10 = $ _____   **7.** $4.08 \div 10 = $ _____

8. $180.4 \div 10 = $ _____   **9.** $1.84 \div 10 = $ _____

Complete.

10. $23.7 \div$ _____ $= 2.37$

11. $0.78 \div$ _____ $= 0.078$

12. _____ $\div 10 = 4.106$

13. _____ $\div 10 = 6.4$

Divide

— Example —

$9 \div 30 = (9 \div \underline{\quad 3 \quad}) \div 10$

$= \underline{\quad 3 \quad} \div 10$

$= \underline{\quad 0.3 \quad}$

So, $9 \div 30 = \underline{\quad 0.3 \quad}$.

14. $0.9 \div 30 = (0.9 \div \underline{\quad\quad}) \div 10$

$= \underline{\quad\quad} \div 10$

$= \underline{\quad\quad}$

So, $0.9 \div 30 = \underline{\quad\quad}$.

15. $0.09 \div 30 = (0.09 \div \underline{\quad\quad}) \div 10$

$= \underline{\quad\quad} \div 10$

$= \underline{\quad\quad}$

So, $0.09 \div 30 = \underline{\quad\quad}$.

16. $1.8 \div 90 = (1.8 \div \underline{\quad\quad}) \div 10$

$= \underline{\quad\quad} \div 10$

$= \underline{\quad\quad}$

So, $1.8 \div 90 = \underline{\quad\quad}$.

Divide.

17.   4.8 ÷ 20 = _____

18.   0.32 ÷ 40 = _____

19.   2.08 ÷ 80 = _____

20.   2.55 ÷ 50 = _____

21.   3.5 ÷ 70 = _____

22.   0.3 ÷ 60 = _____

Divide.

23.   7.5 ÷ 100 = _____

24.   49.3 ÷ 100 = _____

25.   6,001 ÷ 100 = _____

26.   708.2 ÷ 100 = _____

27.   900 ÷ 1,000 = _____

28.   4,103 ÷ 1,000 = _____

29.   909 ÷ 1,000 = _____

30.   9,009 ÷ 1,000 = _____

Complete.

31.   86.2 ÷ _____ = 0.862

32.   275 ÷ _____ = 0.275

33.   _____ ÷ 100 = 0.006

34.   _____ ÷ 1,000 = 3.082

Complete.

┌─ *Example* ──────────────────┐
│   0.07 = 0.7 ÷ __*10*__   │
│   = 7 ÷ __*100*__   │
│   = 70 ÷ __*1,000*__   │
└──────────────────────────────┘

35.   0.31 = 3.1 ÷ _____

          = 31 ÷ _____

          = 310 ÷ _____

36.   8.06 = _____ ÷ 10

          = 806 ÷ _____

          = 8,060 ÷ _____

37.   5.115 = _____ ÷ 10

          = _____ ÷ 100

          = 5,115 ÷ _____

Complete.

Example

$$42 \div 200 = (42 \div \underline{\hspace{0.8cm} 2 \hspace{0.2cm}}) \div 100$$

$$= \underline{\hspace{0.8cm} 21 \hspace{0.2cm}} \div 100$$

$$= \underline{\hspace{0.8cm} 0.21 \hspace{0.2cm}}$$

So, $42 \div 200 = \underline{\hspace{0.8cm} 0.21 \hspace{0.2cm}}$.

---

38. $18.9 \div 900 = (18.9 \div \underline{\hspace{1.5cm}}) \div 100$

$$= \underline{\hspace{1.5cm}} \div 100$$

$$= \underline{\hspace{1.5cm}}$$

So, $18.9 \div 900 = \underline{\hspace{1.5cm}}$.

39. $2 \div 2,000 = (2 \div \underline{\hspace{1.5cm}}) \div 1,000$

$$= \underline{\hspace{1.5cm}} \div 1,000$$

$$= \underline{\hspace{1.5cm}}$$

So, $2 \div 2,000 = \underline{\hspace{1.5cm}}$.

40. $1,500 \div 6,000 = (1,500 \div \underline{\hspace{1.5cm}}) \div 1,000$

$$= \underline{\hspace{1.5cm}} \div 1,000$$

$$= \underline{\hspace{1.5cm}}$$

So, $1,500 \div 6,000 = \underline{\hspace{1.5cm}}$.

Divide.

41. $306 \div 600 = \underline{\hspace{1.5cm}}$ **42.** $29.7 \div 900 = \underline{\hspace{1.5cm}}$

43. $1,056 \div 800 = \underline{\hspace{1.5cm}}$ **44.** $48 \div 2,000 = \underline{\hspace{1.5cm}}$

45. $408 \div 3,000 = \underline{\hspace{1.5cm}}$ **46.** $805 \div 7,000 = \underline{\hspace{1.5cm}}$

Practice 5   Estimating Decimals

**Round each decimal to the nearest whole number.
Then estimate the sum or difference.**

─── *Example* ───

7.7 + 12.3   21.8 − 11.5

7.7 rounds to 8.   21.8 rounds to 22.
12.3 rounds to 12.   11.5 rounds to 12.
8 + 12 = 20   22 − 12 = 10
7.7 + 12.3 is about 20.   21.8 − 11.5 is about 10.

1. $2.90 + $7.15   **2.** 9.05 + 19.55

3. 35.67 − 15.09   **4.** $15.40 − $5.95

Estimate the product by rounding the decimal to the nearest whole number.

Example

4.5 × 4

4.5 rounds to 5.
5 × 4 = 20

4.5 × 4 is about 20.

5. 19.6 × 3

6. 0.95 × 8

7. 8.25 × 3

Estimate the quotient by choosing a whole number close to the dividend that can be evenly divided by the divisor.

Example

24.6 ÷ 5

24.6 is about 25.
25 ÷ 5 = 5

24.6 ÷ 5 is about 5.

8. 38.4 ÷ 6

9. 71.09 ÷ 8

10. 99.75 ÷ 5

Name: ______________________ **Date:** ______________

Round each decimal to the nearest tenth. Then estimate.

11. 0.47 + 15.51

12. 9.95 − 1.46

13. 2.89 pounds × 4

Estimate the quotient by choosing a tenth close to the dividend that can be evenly divided by the divisor.

14. 6.34 kilograms ÷ 7

Solve. Show your work.

15. A bag of walnuts sells for $1.95. Estimate the cost of 8 bags of walnuts.

16. A piece of plywood is 1.27 centimeters thick. Find the thickness of a pile of 9 pieces of plywood to the nearest tenth of a centimeter. Estimate to check if your answer is reasonable.

Practice 6 Converting Metric Units

Convert centimeters to meters or meters to centimeters.

Example

$0.7 \text{ m} = 0.7 \times \underline{\quad 100 \quad}$

$= \underline{\quad 70 \quad} \text{ cm}$

$14.5 \text{ cm} = 14.5 \div \underline{\quad 100 \quad}$

$= \underline{\quad 0.145 \quad} \text{ m}$

Remember, 1 m = 100 cm.

1. $0.9 \text{ m} = 0.9 \times \underline{\qquad}$

$= \underline{\qquad} \text{ cm}$

2. $1.06 \text{ m} = 1.06 \times \underline{\qquad}$

$= \underline{\qquad} \text{ cm}$

3. $3.75 \text{ m} = 3.75 \times \underline{\qquad}$

$= \underline{\qquad} \text{ cm}$

4. $39.23 \text{ m} = 39.23 \times \underline{\qquad}$

$= \underline{\qquad} \text{ cm}$

5. $124 \text{ m} = 124 \times \underline{\qquad}$

$= \underline{\qquad} \text{ cm}$

6. $7.2 \text{ cm} = 7.2 \div \underline{\qquad}$

$= \underline{\qquad} \text{ m}$

7. $180.7 \text{ cm} = 180.7 \div \underline{\qquad}$

$= \underline{\qquad} \text{ m}$

8. $0.6 \text{ cm} = 0.6 \div \underline{\qquad}$

$= \underline{\qquad} \text{ m}$

9. $312 \text{ cm} = 312 \div \underline{\qquad}$

$= \underline{\qquad} \text{ m}$

10. $369.8 \text{ cm} = 369.8 \div \underline{\qquad}$

$= \underline{\qquad} \text{ m}$

Convert meters to meters and centimeters.

Example

9.28 m

0.28 m = 0.28 × ___100___

= ___28___ cm

9.28 m = ___9___ m ___28___ cm

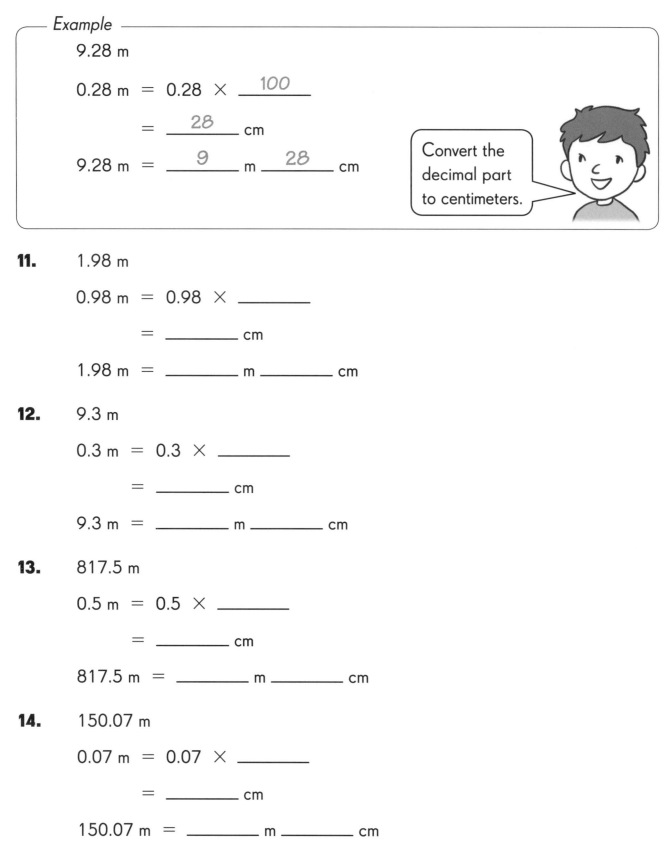

Convert the decimal part to centimeters.

11. 1.98 m

0.98 m = 0.98 × _____

= _____ cm

1.98 m = _____ m _____ cm

12. 9.3 m

0.3 m = 0.3 × _____

= _____ cm

9.3 m = _____ m _____ cm

13. 817.5 m

0.5 m = 0.5 × _____

= _____ cm

817.5 m = _____ m _____ cm

14. 150.07 m

0.07 m = 0.07 × _____

= _____ cm

150.07 m = _____ m _____ cm

Convert meters and centimeters to meters.

┌─ *Example* ───┐

41 m 80 cm

80 cm = 80 ÷ ___100___

      = ___0.8___ m

41 m 80 cm = ___41___ m + ___0.8___ m

          = ___41.8___ m

> First, convert centimeters to meters. Then, combine the two measurements.

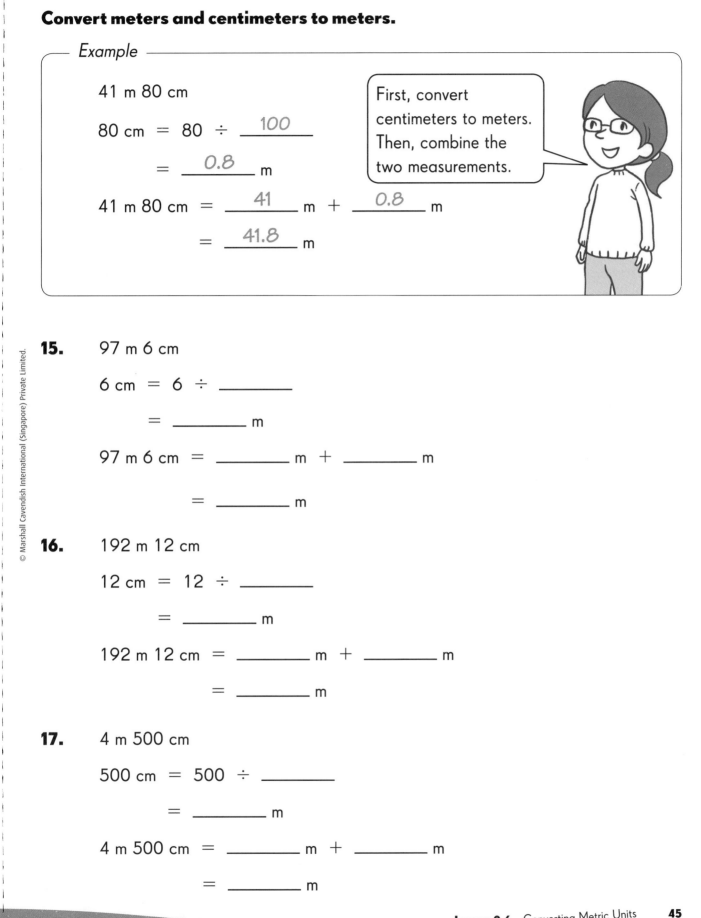

└──┘

15.   97 m 6 cm

6 cm = 6 ÷ _____

      = _____ m

97 m 6 cm = _____ m + _____ m

         = _____ m

16.   192 m 12 cm

12 cm = 12 ÷ _____

      = _____ m

192 m 12 cm = _____ m + _____ m

         = _____ m

17.   4 m 500 cm

500 cm = 500 ÷ _____

      = _____ m

4 m 500 cm = _____ m + _____ m

         = _____ m

18.   7 m 7 cm

   7 cm = 7 ÷ _____

   = _____ m

   7 m 7 cm = _____ m + _____ m

   = _____ m

Convert meters to kilometers or kilometers to meters.

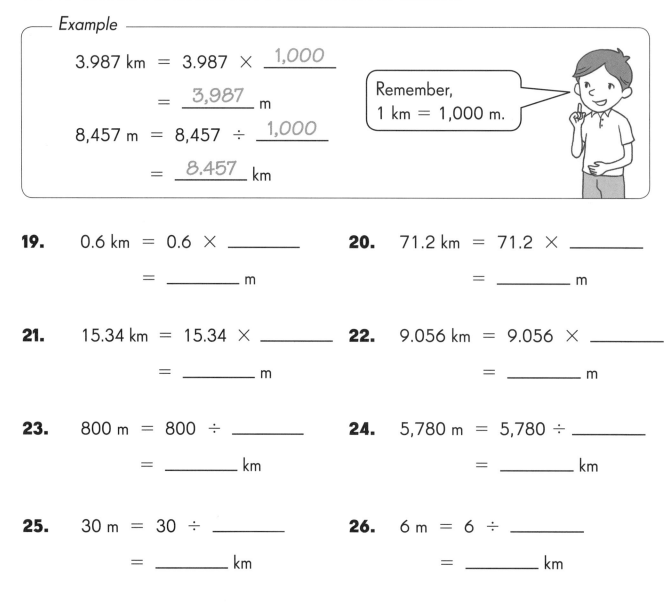

Example

3.987 km = 3.987 × _1,000_

= _3,987_ m

8,457 m = 8,457 ÷ _1,000_

= _8.457_ km

Remember,
1 km = 1,000 m.

19.   0.6 km = 0.6 × _____

= _____ m

20.   71.2 km = 71.2 × _____

= _____ m

21.   15.34 km = 15.34 × _____

= _____ m

22.   9.056 km = 9.056 × _____

= _____ m

23.   800 m = 800 ÷ _____

= _____ km

24.   5,780 m = 5,780 ÷ _____

= _____ km

25.   30 m = 30 ÷ _____

= _____ km

26.   6 m = 6 ÷ _____

= _____ km

Convert grams to kilograms or kilograms to grams.

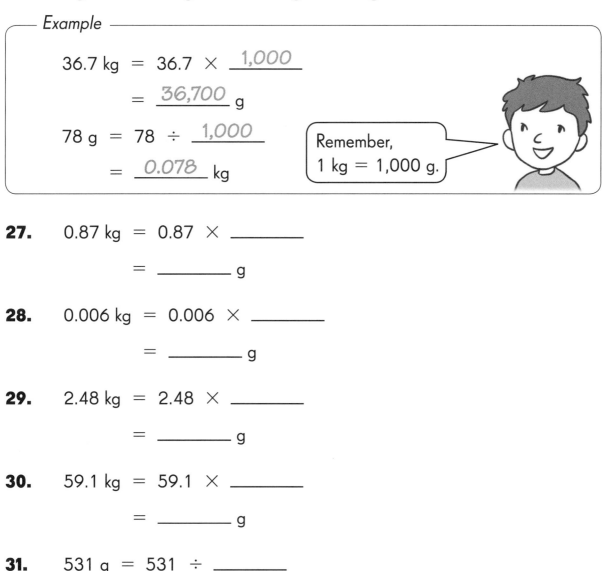

Example

$36.7 \text{ kg} = 36.7 \times \underline{1,000}$

$= \underline{36,700} \text{ g}$

$78 \text{ g} = 78 \div \underline{1,000}$

$= \underline{0.078} \text{ kg}$

Remember,
1 kg = 1,000 g.

27. $0.87 \text{ kg} = 0.87 \times \underline{\hspace{2cm}}$

$= \underline{\hspace{2cm}} \text{ g}$

28. $0.006 \text{ kg} = 0.006 \times \underline{\hspace{2cm}}$

$= \underline{\hspace{2cm}} \text{ g}$

29. $2.48 \text{ kg} = 2.48 \times \underline{\hspace{2cm}}$

$= \underline{\hspace{2cm}} \text{ g}$

30. $59.1 \text{ kg} = 59.1 \times \underline{\hspace{2cm}}$

$= \underline{\hspace{2cm}} \text{ g}$

31. $531 \text{ g} = 531 \div \underline{\hspace{2cm}}$

$= \underline{\hspace{2cm}} \text{ kg}$

32. $2 \text{ g} = 2 \div \underline{\hspace{2cm}}$

$= \underline{\hspace{2cm}} \text{ kg}$

33. $61,900 \text{ g} = 61,900 \div \underline{\hspace{2cm}}$

$= \underline{\hspace{2cm}} \text{ kg}$

Convert milliliters to liters or liters to milliliters.

Example

3.975 L $= 3.975 \times$ _1,000_

$=$ _3,975_ mL

550 mL $= 550 \div$ _1,000_

$=$ _0.55_ L

Remember,
1 L = 1,000 mL.

---

34. 2.09 L $= 2.09 \times$ _____

$=$ _____ mL

35. 0.054 L $= 0.054 \times$ _____

$=$ _____ mL

36. 13.9 L $= 13.9 \times$ _____

$=$ _____ mL

37. 1.4 L $= 1.4 \times$ _____

$=$ _____ mL

38. 58.12 L $= 58.12 \times$ _____

$=$ _____ mL

39. 940 mL $= 940 \div$ _____

$=$ _____ L

40. $8,500$ mL $= 8,500 \div$ _____

$=$ _____ L

41. 917 mL $= 917 \div$ _____

$=$ _____ L

42. 25 mL $= 25 \div$ _____

$=$ _____ L

43. $3,575$ mL $= 3,575 \div$ _____

$=$ _____ L

Convert each measurement.

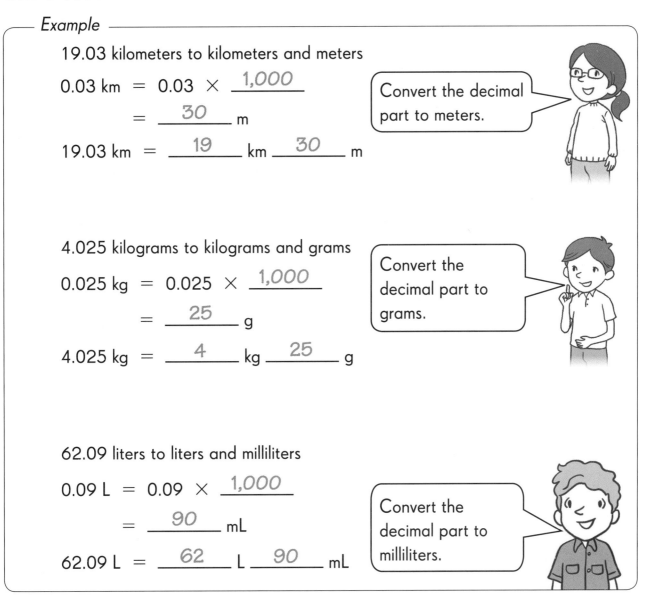

Example

19.03 kilometers to kilometers and meters

0.03 km = 0.03 × __1,000__

= __30__ m

19.03 km = __19__ km __30__ m

Convert the decimal part to meters.

4.025 kilograms to kilograms and grams

0.025 kg = 0.025 × __1,000__

= __25__ g

4.025 kg = __4__ kg __25__ g

Convert the decimal part to grams.

62.09 liters to liters and milliliters

0.09 L = 0.09 × __1,000__

= __90__ mL

62.09 L = __62__ L __90__ mL

Convert the decimal part to milliliters.

44.   0.73 kilometer to kilometers and meters

0.73 km = 0.73 × _____

= _____ m

0.73 km = _____ km _____ m

45. 90.04 kilometers to kilometers and meters

0.04 km = 0.04 × _____

= _____ m

90.04 km = _____ km _____ m

46. 1.008 kilometers to kilometers and meters

0.008 km = 0.008 × _____

= _____ m

1.008 km = _____ km _____ m

47. 50.05 kilometers to kilometers and meters

0.05 km = 0.05 × _____

= _____ m

50.05 km = _____ km _____ m

48. 15.3 kilograms to kilograms and grams

0.3 kg = 0.3 × _____

= _____ g

15.3 kg = _____ kg _____ g

49. 20.05 kilograms to kilograms and grams

0.05 kg = 0.05 × _____

= _____ g

20.05 kg = _____ kg _____ g

50. 8.214 kilograms to kilograms and grams

0.214 kg = 0.214 ✕ _____

= _____ g

8.214 kg = _____ kg _____ g

51. 7.09 liters to liters and milliliters

0.09 L = 0.09 ✕ _____

= _____ mL

7.09 L = _____ L _____ mL

52. 66.8 liters to liters and milliliters

0.8 L = 0.8 ✕ _____

= _____ mL

66.8 L = _____ L _____ mL

53. 867.001 liters to liters and milliliters

0.001 L = 0.001 ✕ _____

= _____ mL

867.001 L = _____ L _____ mL

Convert each measurement.

Example

9 kilometers 8 meters to kilometers

8 m = 8 ÷ __1,000__

= __0.008__ km

> First, convert meters to kilometers. Then, combine the two measurements.

9 km 8 m = __9__ km + __0.008__ km

= __9.008__ km

---

12 kilograms 510 grams to kilograms

510 g = 510 ÷ __1,000__

= __0.51__ kg

> First, convert grams to kilograms. Then, combine the two measurements.

12 kg 510 g = __12__ kg + __0.51__ kg

= __12.51__ kg

---

4 liters 25 milliliters to liters

25 mL = 25 ÷ __1,000__

= __0.025__ L

> First, convert milliliters to liters. Then, combine the two measurements.

4 L 25 mL = __4__ L + __0.025__ L

= __4.025__ L

54.   25 kilometers 80 meters to kilometers

80 m = 80 ÷ _____

= _____ km

25 km 80 m = _____ km + _____ km

= _____ km

55.   17 kilometers 6 meters to kilometers

6 m = 6 ÷ _____

= _____ km

17 km 6 m = _____ km + _____ km

= _____ km

56.   7 kilometers 35 meters to kilometers

35 m = 35 ÷ _____

= _____ km

7 km 35 m = _____ km + _____ km

= _____ km

57.   41 kilometers 990 meters to kilometers

990 m = 990 ÷ _____

= _____ km

41 km 990 m = _____ km + _____ km

= _____ km

58. 5 kilograms 73 grams to kilograms

$73 \text{ g} = 73 \div$ _____

$= $ _____ kg

$5 \text{ kg } 73 \text{ g} = $ _____ kg $+$ _____ kg

$= $ _____ kg

59. 10 kilograms 5 grams to kilograms

$5 \text{ g} = 5 \div$ _____

$= $ _____ kg

$10 \text{ kg } 5 \text{ g} = $ _____ kg $+$ _____ kg

$= $ _____ kg

60. 90 liters 70 milliliters to liters

$70 \text{ mL} = 70 \div$ _____

$= $ _____ L

$90 \text{ L } 70 \text{ mL} = $ _____ L $+$ _____ L

$= $ _____ L

61. 58 liters 650 milliliters to liters

$650 \text{ mL} = 650 \div$ _____

$= $ _____ L

$58 \text{ L } 650 \text{ mL} = $ _____ L $+$ _____ L

$= $ _____ L

Solve. Show your work.

62. William runs 5 meters in 20 steps. How many kilometers will he run after taking 1,000 steps?

63. A bottle of fruit juice is 800 milliliters. How many liters of fruit juice are in 120 bottles?

64. A box weighs 750 grams. There are 25 such boxes. What is the total weight of the boxes in kilograms? Give your answer to the nearest tenth.

65. Trees are planted along a road that is 2 kilometers 50 meters long. Eleven trees are planted at an equal distance apart along the road. What is the distance in meters between each tree?

Practice 7   Real-World Problems: Decimals

Solve. Show your work.

1.   How many liters of spring water are in six bottles if each bottle contains 0.33 liter of spring water? Round your answer to the nearest liter.

2.   A plumber has a copper pipe 0.9 meter long. He cuts the pipe into four equal pieces. Find the length of each piece in meters. Round your answer to the nearest tenth of a meter.

3.   Ashton is thinking of a number. When she divides it by 7, she gets a quotient of 7.35. What number is Ashton thinking of?

Solve. Show your work.

4. Mr. Kasac drives 32.27 miles from his office to his home. After driving 15.65 miles, he stopped at the dry cleaner's. How much farther does he have to drive before he gets home? Round your answer to the nearest mile.

5. 4 gallons of low fat milk cost $13.80. Find the cost of 6 gallons of low fat milk.

6. 3 cans of green beans cost $1.80. Rizal bought 9 cans of green beans. How much did he pay?

Solve. Show your work.

7.   During the summer, Andrew worked for 5 days each week. He worked
8 hours each day. In a week, he earned $360. How much was he paid
for each hour of work?

8.   A bag contains 10 pounds of dog food. A family feeds their dogs
0.85 pound of dog food a day. How much dog food is left in the bag
after 7 days? Round your answer to the nearest pound.

Solve. Show your work.

9. A box of rice cakes costs $1.95. What is the greatest number of boxes of rice cakes Jared can buy with $10?

10. A metal rod 9.4 meters long is cut into two pieces. One piece is 3 times as long as the other. Find the length of the longer piece in meters. Round your answer to the nearest tenth of a meter.

Solve. Show your work.

11. Rani bought 9 similar notebooks. She gave the cashier $10 and received change of $5.05. What was the cost of 1 notebook?

12. A kilogram of whole-wheat flour costs $6. What is the cost of 400 grams of the flour?

Solve. Show your work.

13. A shop owner bought 30 folders and some journals. He paid $82.50 for the folders. Each journal cost 10 times as much as a folder. What was the cost of each journal?

14. There are 1,000 workers in a factory. Each worker works 30 hours a week and is paid $10.50 an hour. How much does the company pay the workers altogether each week?

Practice 8 Real-World Problems: Decimals

Solve. Show your work.

1. Mrs. Lee uses 0.025 kilogram of wax to make a candle.
On Monday, she made 50 candles. On Tuesday, she made 4 times as
many candles as on Monday. How much wax did she use to make the
candles on Tuesday?

2. One lap of a race track measures 4.68 kilometers. During a race of
56 laps, a driver stops to refuel after completing 48 laps. How many
more kilometers does he have to drive to finish the race?

Solve. Show your work.

3. Mrs. Rahlee bought 300 yards of ribbon to make flowers. She used
    1.22 yards to make one large flower. She made 200 such large flowers
    She used all of the remaining ribbon to make 100 small flowers.
    What was the length of ribbon Mrs. Rahlee used to make one small flower?

4. Britta bought some carrots and apples for $24.80. A carrot and an
    apple cost $0.90 altogether. She bought more carrots than apples.
    The cost of the extra number of carrots was $6.80. How many apples
    did Britta buy?

Solve. Show your work.

5. A plastic tub has a capacity of 13.5 quarts. It can hold 3 times as much liquid as a pail. The pail can hold twice as much liquid as a can. Find the capacity of the pail and that of the can in quarts.

6. Marcy paid $35 for 10 kilograms of raisins. She divided the raisins equally into two containers. Then she sold the raisins in the first container at $4.50 per kilogram and those in the second container at $5.50 per kilogram. How much money did Marcy earn after selling all the raisins?

Math Journal

Solve. Show your work.

1. James has a square piece of paper. He wants to cut it into 20 strips of equal width.
    He says, 'This piece of paper is **about** 48 centimeters wide.'
    How can he find out the width of each strip without measuring?
    Is this width accurate?

2. James takes a ruler and measures the width of the piece of paper.
    He finds that the actual width is 48.8 centimeters.
    Find the width of each strip. How can you check if your answer
    is reasonable?

Put On Your Thinking Cap!

Challenging Practice

Solve. Show your work.

1. A plumber has two pipes. One pipe is 7 times as long as the other pipe. She cuts 2.2 meters from the longer pipe. The remaining length of this pipe is 3 times that of the shorter pipe. Find the length of the shorter pipe in meters.

2. At a farmer's market, 5 pounds of strawberries cost $21.50. At a supermarket, 3 pounds of the same quality strawberries cost $15.75.

    a. Which is a better buy?

    b. How much can you save by buying 20 pounds of the strawberries that are the better buy?

Put On Your Thinking Cap!

Problem Solving

Solve. Show your work.

1. Sam buys 10 oranges and 11 apples for $10.05. The total cost of 1 orange and 1 apple is $0.94. How much does an apple cost?

2. A bucket filled with sand has a mass of 11.15 kilograms. When it is filled with water, the mass is 5.95 kilograms. The mass of the sand is twice that of the water. Find the mass of the bucket in grams.

Solve. Show your work.

3. The total capacity of 6 pitchers and 12 glasses is 21 liters. The capacity of a pitcher is 5 times that of a glass. Find the capacity of each glass. Give your answer in liters.

Solve. Show your work.

4.   Dahlia has just enough money to buy either 6 pears and 20 oranges or 12 oranges and 11 pears. A pear costs $0.80. How much does an orange cost?

Percent

Practice 1   Percent

Each large square is divided into 100 parts.
Fill in the blanks to describe each large square.

1.

_____ out of 100 equal parts are shaded.

_____% of the large square is shaded.

_____ out of 100 equal parts are not shaded.

_____% of the large square is not shaded.

2.

_____ out of 100 equal parts are shaded.

_____% of the large square is shaded.

_____ out of 100 equal parts are not shaded.

_____% of the large square is not shaded.

Express each fraction as a percent.

> **Example**
>
> $\frac{38}{100} = \underline{\quad 38 \quad}\%$

3. $\frac{92}{100} = \underline{\hspace{2cm}}\%$

4. $\frac{7}{100} = \underline{\hspace{2cm}}\%$

5. $\frac{19}{100} = \underline{\hspace{2cm}}\%$

6. $\frac{6}{10} = \underline{\hspace{2cm}}\%$

7. $\frac{4}{10} = \underline{\hspace{2cm}}\%$

Express each decimal as a percent.

> **Example**
>
> $0.15 = \dfrac{\boxed{15}}{100}$
>
> $ = \underline{\quad 15 \quad}\%$

8. $0.28 = \dfrac{\boxed{}}{100}$

$ = \underline{\hspace{2cm}}\%$

9. $0.07 = \underline{\hspace{2cm}}\%$

10. $0.01 = \underline{\hspace{2cm}}\%$

11. $0.08 = \underline{\hspace{2cm}}\%$

12. $0.5 = \underline{\hspace{2cm}}\%$

13. $0.9 = \underline{\hspace{2cm}}\%$

14. $0.8 = \underline{\hspace{2cm}}\%$

Express each percent as a fraction with a denominator of 100.

> **Example**
>
> $53\% = \dfrac{\boxed{53}}{100}$

15. $7\% = \dfrac{\boxed{}}{100}$

16. $13\% = \boxed{}$

17. $31\% = \boxed{}$

18. $5\% = \boxed{}$

19. $79\% = \boxed{}$

Express each percent as a fraction in simplest form.

Example

$5\% = \dfrac{\boxed{5}}{100}$

$= \boxed{\dfrac{1}{20}}$

20. $25\% = \dfrac{\boxed{}}{100}$

$= \boxed{}$

21. $75\% = \boxed{}$

22. $84\% = \boxed{}$

23. $46\% = \boxed{}$

24. $55\% = \boxed{}$

Express each percent as a decimal.

Example

$27\% = \dfrac{\boxed{27}}{100}$

$= \underline{\ \ 0.27\ \ }$

25. $58\% = \dfrac{\boxed{}}{100}$

$= \underline{}$

26. $9\% = \underline{}$

27. $1\% = \underline{}$

Write each ratio as a fraction and then as a percent.

		As a Fraction	As a Percent
28.	23 out of 100		
29.	9 out of 10		

Express each percent as a decimal. Then mark X to show where each decimal is located on the number line.

30.   71% = _____   **31.**   19% = _____   **32.**   44% = _____

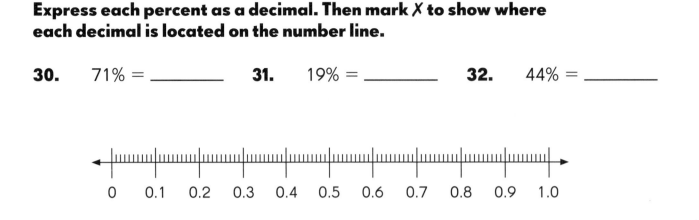

Solve. Show your work.

33.   There are 100 students in a drawing contest, and 58 of them are girls.

    a.   What percent of the students in the contest are girls?

    b.   What percent of the students in the contest are boys?

34.   A jogging route is 10 kilometers long. Lee Ming has jogged 4 kilometers of the route.

    a.   What percent of the route has Lee Ming jogged?

    b.   What percent of the route does Lee Ming have to jog to complete the whole route?

Practice 2   Expressing Fractions as Percents

Express each fraction as a percent.

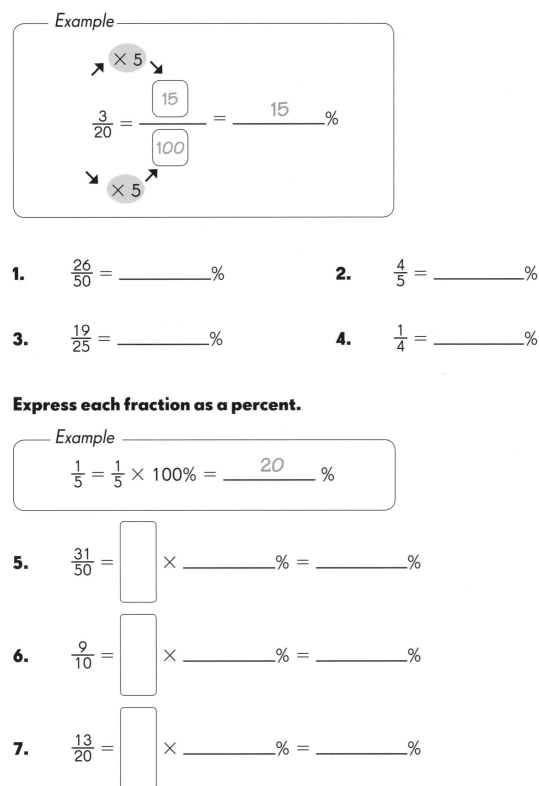

Example

$$\frac{3}{20} = \frac{15}{100} = \underline{\quad 15 \quad}\%$$

(×5 / ×5)

1. $\frac{26}{50} = $ _____ %

2. $\frac{4}{5} = $ _____ %

3. $\frac{19}{25} = $ _____ %

4. $\frac{1}{4} = $ _____ %

Express each fraction as a percent.

Example

$$\frac{1}{5} = \frac{1}{5} \times 100\% = \underline{\quad 20 \quad}\%$$

5. $\frac{31}{50} = $ [   ] × _____ % = _____ %

6. $\frac{9}{10} = $ [   ] × _____ % = _____ %

7. $\frac{13}{20} = $ [   ] × _____ % = _____ %

**Express each fraction as a percent.
Use the model to help you.**

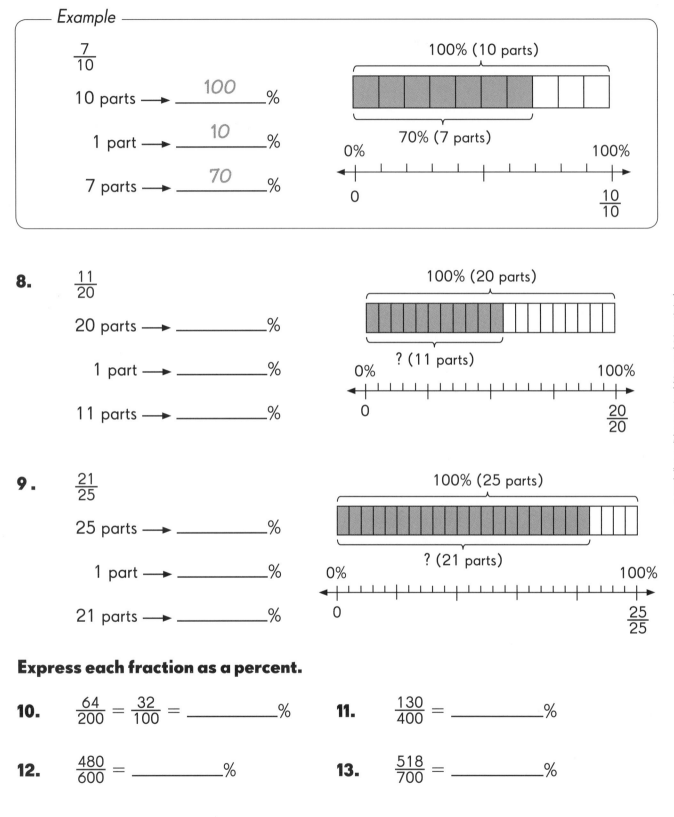

Example

$\frac{7}{10}$

10 parts ⟶ ___100___%

1 part ⟶ ___10___%

7 parts ⟶ ___70___%

100% (10 parts)

70% (7 parts)

0%   100%

0 $\frac{10}{10}$

8. $\frac{11}{20}$

20 parts ⟶ _____%

1 part ⟶ _____%

11 parts ⟶ _____%

100% (20 parts)

? (11 parts)

0%   100%

0 $\frac{20}{20}$

9. $\frac{21}{25}$

25 parts ⟶ _____%

1 part ⟶ _____%

21 parts ⟶ _____%

100% (25 parts)

? (21 parts)

0%   100%

0 $\frac{25}{25}$

Express each fraction as a percent.

10. $\frac{64}{200} = \frac{32}{100} =$ _____%

11. $\frac{130}{400} =$ _____%

12. $\frac{480}{600} =$ _____%

13. $\frac{518}{700} =$ _____%

Solve. Show your work.

14. Jeremy finished $\frac{3}{5}$ of his homework. What percent of his homework did he finish?

15. Tracy ran in a marathon, but managed to complete only $\frac{13}{20}$ of the race.

a. What percent of the marathon did she complete?

b. What percent of the marathon did she not complete?

Solve. Show your work.

16. Katie bought some flour. She used $\frac{3}{8}$ of it to bake bread. What percent of the flour is left?

17. There are 800 members in an astronomy club, and 320 of them are females. What percent of the members are males?

Practice 3   Percent of a Number

Multiply.

1.   25% × 84 = _____

2.   36% × 75 = _____

3.   40% of 680 = _____

4.   55% of 720 = _____

Solve. Show your work.

5.   Of the 240 shirts on a rack, 40% are size medium.
How many shirts on the rack are size medium?

240 shirts

?(40%)

Solve. Show your work.

6. There are 720 students in a school. One rainy day, 5% of the students were absent. How many students were absent?

5% of 720 = ?

7. Jenny made 200 bracelets. She sold 64% of the bracelets at a craft fair.

a. How many bracelets did she sell?

b. How many bracelets were not sold?

Solve. Show your work.

8. There were 12,000 spectators in one section of the stadium. In that section, 55% had on red shirts and the rest had on white shirts. How many spectators had on white shirts?

9. Mrs. Patel went shopping with $120. She spent 12% of the money on meat, and 25% on vegetables. How much money did she have left?

Solve. Show your work.

10. A vendor sells three types of watches. Of the watches in stock, 20% are men's watches, 40% are ladies' watches, and the rest are children's watches. There are 250 watches altogether. How many children's watches are there?

Practice 4   Real-World Problems: Percent

Solve. Show your work.

1.   Jennifer bought a printer that cost $240. There was a 7% sales tax on the printer.

   a.   How much sales tax did Jennifer pay?

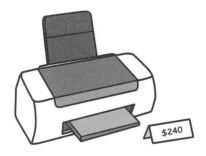

$240

   b.   How much did Jennifer pay for the printer with tax?

2.   A company invests $8,000 in an account that pays 6% interest per year.

   a.   How much interest will the company earn at the end of 1 year?

   b.   How much money will the company have in the account at the end of 1 year?

Solve. Show your work.

3. The regular price of a digital camera was $250. Tyrone bought the digital camera at a discount of 40%. How much did Tyrone pay for the digital camera?

4. Len bought a new car for $22,500. After a few years, he sold the car at a discount of 25%. What was the selling price of the car?

Solve. Show your work.

5. The price for dinner in a restaurant was $80. The customer paid an additional 7% meals tax and left a $15 tip.

    a. How much meals tax did the customer pay?

    b. How much did the customer spend altogether in the restaurant?

6. The regular price of a pair of hockey skates was $250. Ron bought the skates at a discount of 8%. However, he had to pay 5% sales tax on the skates after the discount.

    a. What was the selling price of the skates?

    b. How much did Ron pay for the skates in total?

Math Journal

Arnold had dinner at a restaurant with his family. The dinner cost $72. In addition, he paid 7% meals tax on the dinner. How much did Arnold pay for the dinner?

Tyrone worked out the answer using his calculator like this:

93% × $72 = $66.96

Brandon worked out the answer using his calculator like this:

107% × $72 = $77.04

Whose answer is correct? Explain why his answer is correct.

Put On Your Thinking Cap!

Challenging Practice

Solve. Show your work.

1. Mr. Stanton bought a cell phone at 80% of the regular price. The regular price of the phone was $450. Mr. Wilson bought the same cell phone but paid $500 for it. How much more did Mr. Wilson pay than Mr. Stanton?

2. Helen has 30 tickets. Gina has 20 more tickets than Helen. What percent of her tickets must Gina give Helen so that both of them have the same number of tickets?

Put On Your Thinking Cap!

Problem Solving

Solve. Show your work.

Michelle collects U.S., Canadian, and Mexican stamps. In her collection, 80% of the stamps are U.S. and Mexican stamps. There are 3 times as many U.S. stamps as Mexican stamps. What percent of Michelle's collection is made up of U.S. stamps?

Concepts and Skills

Mark X to show where each decimal is located on the number line. *(Lesson 8.1)*

1.   0.032   **2.**   0.047

0.03   0.04   0.05

Complete. *(Lesson 8.1)*

3.   3 tenths 5 hundredths = _____ thousandths

4.   803 thousandths = _____ tenths _____ thousandths

5.   0.835 = 8 tenths 3 hundredths _____ thousandths

Write the equivalent decimal. *(Lesson 8.1)*

6.   8 ones and 214 thousandths = _____

7.   1,180 thousandths = _____

8. $7\frac{60}{1000}$ = _____

9. $\frac{6050}{1000}$ = _____

4.526 can be written in expanded form as 4 + 0.5 + 0.02 + 0.006. Write each decimal in expanded notation. *(Lesson 8.1)*

10. $\quad 0.329 = $ _____ + _____ + _____

11. $\quad 20.125 = $ _____ + _____ + _____ + _____

Complete. *(Lesson 8.1)*

In 9.168,

12. $\quad$ the digit 6 is in the _____ place.

13. $\quad$ the value of the digit 8 is _____.

14. $\quad$ the digit 1 stands for _____.

Compare. Write >, <, or =. *(Lesson 8.2)*

15. $\quad$ 1.07 $\bigcirc$ 1.7

16. $\quad$ 3.562 $\bigcirc$ 3.526

17. $\quad$ 15.4 $\bigcirc$ 15.40

Order the decimals. *(Lesson 8.2)*

18. $\quad$ 2.08, 1.973, 6.1

$\quad$ Begin with the least:

_____

19. $\quad$ 1.567, 1.667, 1.376

$\quad$ Begin with the greatest:

_____

Fill in the blanks. *(Lesson 8.2)*

20.   The mass of a strand of hair is 0.179 gram.

Round the mass to the nearest hundredth of a gram.

0.179 gram rounds to _____ gram.

21.   The length of a rope is 2.589 yards.

Round the length to the nearest tenth of a yard.

2.589 yards rounds to _____ yards.

Write each decimal as a mixed number in simplest form. *(Lesson 8.3)*

22. $6.2 =$ _____

23. $2.16 =$ _____

Multiply. *(Lessons 9.1 and 9.2)*

24. $29.3 \times 8 =$ _____

25. $12.08 \times 5 =$ _____

26. $86.4 \times 10 =$ _____

27. $13.5 \times 30 =$ _____

28. $73.96 \times 100 =$ _____

29. $6.2 \times 700 =$ _____

30. $9.34 \times 1,000 = $ _____

31. $25.6 \times 9,000 = $ _____

Multiply. *(Lesson 9.2)*

32. $7.8 \times 10^2 = $ _____

33. $0.05 \times 10^3 = $ _____

34. $0.178 \times 10^2 = $ _____

35. $9.5 \times 10^3 = $ _____

36. $20.1 \times 10^2 = $ _____

37. $1.206 \times 10^3 = $ _____

Divide. *(Lesson 9.3)*

38. 0.5 ÷ 5 = _____

39. 0.63 ÷ 9 = _____

40. 36.8 ÷ 4 = _____

41. 96.3 ÷ 5 = _____

42. 3.36 ÷ 4 = _____

43. 1.92 ÷ 8 = _____

Divide. Round the quotient to the nearest tenth and nearest hundredth. *(Lesson 9.3)*

44. 19 ÷ 7 = _____ to the nearest tenth

   19 ÷ 7 = _____ to the nearest hundredth

Divide. (*Lesson 9.4*)

45. $38 \div 10 = $ _____

46. $19.6 \div 20 = $ _____

47. $4.5 \div 100 = $ _____

48. $375 \div 300 = $ _____

49. $5,030 \div 1,000 = $ _____

50. $2,506 \div 7,000 = $ _____

Estimate each answer by rounding the numbers to an appropriate place. (*Lesson 9.5*)

51. $91.2 + 25.9$

52. $37.4 - 11.7$

53. 21.63×5

54. $7.55 \div 8$

Convert. *(Lesson 9.6)*

55. 3.5 m = _____ cm

56. 61.9 m = _____ m _____ cm

57. 9.072 km = _____ m

58. 15.8 km = _____ km _____ m

59. 0.07 kg = _____ g

60. 59.06 kg = _____ kg _____ g

61. 70.4 L = _____ mL

62. 2.007 L = _____ L _____ mL

Convert. *(Lesson 9.6)*

63. 73.9 cm = _____ m   **64.** 5 m 12 cm = _____ m

65. 79 m = _____ km   **66.** 40 km 56 m = _____ km

67. 6 g = _____ kg   **68.** 81,500 mL = _____ L

Write each ratio in three ways. Complete the table. (*Lesson 10.1*)

		As a Fraction	As a Percent	As a Decimal
69.	57 out of 100			
70.	8 out of 10			

Express each fraction as a percent. (*Lesson 10.2*)

71. $\dfrac{88}{200} =$

72. $\dfrac{204}{400} =$

73. $\dfrac{6}{20} =$

74. $\dfrac{7}{50} =$

75. $\dfrac{13}{20} =$

76. $\dfrac{16}{25} =$

Problem Solving

Solve. Show your work.

77. Hazel saves $5.75 each week. How much does she save in 2 weeks?

78. Tyrone spends $23.83 on a book and $9.12 on a wallet. How much does he spend on the two items?

79. Evelyn has 12.7 quarts of fruit punch in a cooler. She pours the fruit punch into glasses. She fills 5 glasses, each with a capacity of 0.36 quart. Then she fills 8 glasses, each with a capacity of 0.52 quart. How much fruit punch is left in the cooler?

Solve. Use models to help you.

80. The total weight of three tables is 16.9 pounds. The first table is twice as heavy as the second table. The weight of the third table is $\frac{1}{3}$ the weight of the second table. What is the weight of the first table?

81. There are 950 seats in a theater. 82% of the seats are occupied. How many seats are not occupied?

Solve. Use models to help you.

82. Rahim spends 10% of his weekly allowance on Monday. On Wednesday, he spends $\frac{1}{3}$ of the remainder. What percent of his allowance is left at the end of Wednesday?

83. Ms. Jones buys a violin for $860. In addition, she has to pay 7% sales tax. How much does she pay in all?

84. The length of a table is 2.1 meters long. It is 7 times as long as the length of a square paper. What is the perimeter of the paper? Give your answers in centimeters.

Solve. Show your work.

85. The regular price of a television set is $1,200. Albert buys the television set at a discount of 35%. How much does he pay for the television set?

86. A school band gives a year-end concert. It is held in a 400-seat auditorium. Each concert ticket sells for $10, and 85% of the tickets are sold. How much money does the band earn from the sale of the tickets?

87. Mr. Aaron's luggage weighs 25.97 kilograms. How much more can he pack if he is allowed to bring 30 kilograms? Give your answer in kilograms and grams.

Chapter

11 Graphs and Probability

Practice 1 Making and Interpreting Line Plots

Use the data in the table to answer the questions.

Example

Marco has strips of wires of different lengths, as shown in the table below.

Length of Strips (m)	$\frac{1}{5}$	$\frac{2}{5}$	$\frac{3}{5}$	$\frac{7}{10}$
Number of Strips	3	1	6	5

Marco made a line plot to show the number of strips. Each ✗ represents one strip.

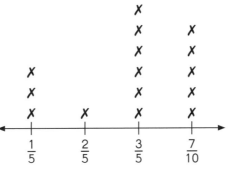

Strips of Wire

1. What is the total length of the strips of wire?

$$3 \times \frac{1}{5} + 1 \times \frac{2}{5} + 6 \times \frac{3}{5} + 5 \times \frac{7}{10} = \frac{81}{10} = 8\frac{1}{10}$$

The total length is $\frac{8}{10}$ meter.

2. Marco uses 3 of the $\frac{3}{5}$-meter strips to make a doll. What is the total length of wire needed to make a doll?

$$3 \times \frac{3}{5} = \frac{9}{5} = 1\frac{4}{5}$$

Marco uses $1\frac{4}{5}$ meters to make a doll.

Use the data in the table to answer the questions.

The table below shows the amount of orange juice in 9 juice boxes.

Amount of Orange Juice (pt)	$\frac{1}{4}$	$\frac{3}{8}$	$\frac{1}{2}$	$\frac{5}{8}$
Number of Juice Boxes	2	2	4	1

1. Make a line plot to show the data in the table.

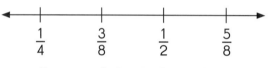

$$\frac{1}{4} \qquad \frac{3}{8} \qquad \frac{1}{2} \qquad \frac{5}{8}$$

Orange Juice in Juice Boxes

2. What is the total amount of orange juice in all of the juice boxes?

The total amount of juice is _____.

3. All the orange juice is poured equally into 5 containers. How much juice is in each container?

The amount of juice in each container is _____.

Use the data in the table to answer the questions.

Kelly weighs some lumps of clay and records their weight in a table, as shown below.

Weight of Clay Lumps (lb)	$\frac{1}{8}$	$\frac{1}{4}$	$\frac{1}{2}$	$\frac{5}{8}$	$\frac{7}{8}$
Number of Clay Lumps	3	3	2	1	1

4. Make a line plot to show the data given in the table.

$$\frac{1}{8} \qquad \frac{1}{4} \qquad \frac{1}{2} \qquad \frac{5}{8} \qquad \frac{7}{8}$$

Weight of Clay Lumps

5. What is the total weight for each group of weight of clay lumps?

6. Which weight group of lumps ($\frac{1}{8}$, $\frac{1}{4}$, $\frac{1}{2}$, $\frac{5}{8}$, or $\frac{7}{8}$) had the greatest total weight?

The group of lumps that had the greatest total weight was _____.

Which weight group of lumps had the least weight?

The group of lumps that had the least total weight was _____.

7. The lumps of clay are combined and then divided into 10 lumps of equal weight. What is the weight of each new lump of clay?

The weight of each new lump is = _____.

Use the data in the table to answer the questions.

Rectangular tiles of different sizes were used to make an art piece. The table shows the area of the tiles that were used.

Area of Rectangular Tiles (ft²)	$\frac{3}{8}$	$\frac{9}{16}$	$\frac{3}{4}$
Number of Tiles	3	4	2

8.   Make a line plot to show the data in the table.

9. What is the total area of the art piece when all the tiles are fitted together?

The total area of the art piece is _____.

10. The weight of 1 square foot of tile is 10 ounces. What is the weight of the entire art piece?

The weight of the entire art piece is _____.

Practice 2 Making and Interpreting Double Bar Graphs

Complete. Use the data in the graph.

The double bar graph shows the number of boys and girls in two classes, 5A and 5B.

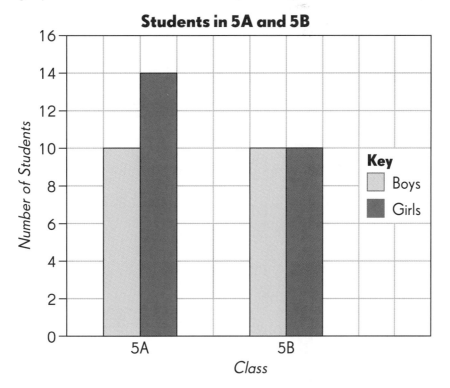

Students in 5A and 5B

Number of Students / Class

Key
Boys
Girls

1. There are _____ students in 5A and _____ students in 5B.

2. There are _____ more girls than boys in 5A.

3. Class _____ has an equal number of boys and girls.

4. There are _____ girls altogether in 5A and 5B.

5. There are _____ boys altogether in 5A and 5B.

6. The average number of students in the two classes is _____.

Complete the bar graph using the data in the table. Then answer the questions.

7. The table shows the number of bags of apples and oranges sold by a grocer in three days.

	Thursday	Friday	Saturday
Number of Bags of Apples	20	25	30
Number of Bags of Oranges	25	35	45

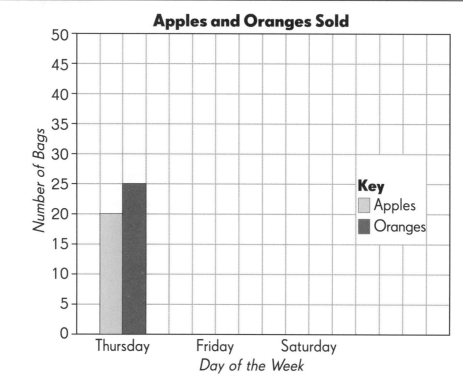

8. On Friday, _____ more bags of oranges than apples were sold.

9. On Saturday, _____ fewer bags of apples than oranges were sold.

10. The total number of bags of apples and oranges sold was the greatest on

_____.

11. The difference between the number of bags of apples and oranges sold

was the least on _____.

Practice 3   Graphing an Equation

Write the ordered pair for each point.

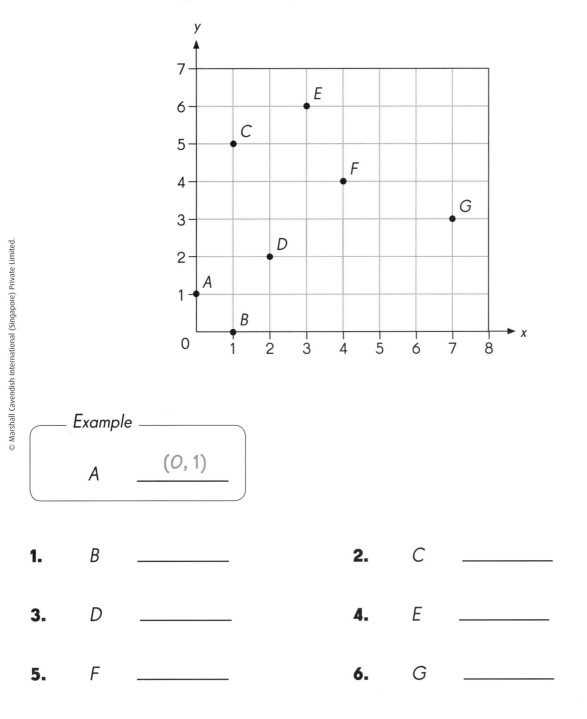

Example

A _____(0, 1)_____

---

1.   B _____   **2.**   C _____

3.   D _____   **4.**   E _____

5.   F _____   **6.**   G _____

Plot each point on the coordinate grid.

7.   P (0, 5)

8.   Q (4, 0)

9.   R (3, 6)

10.   S (5, 1)

11.   T (2, 5)

12.   U (0, 0)

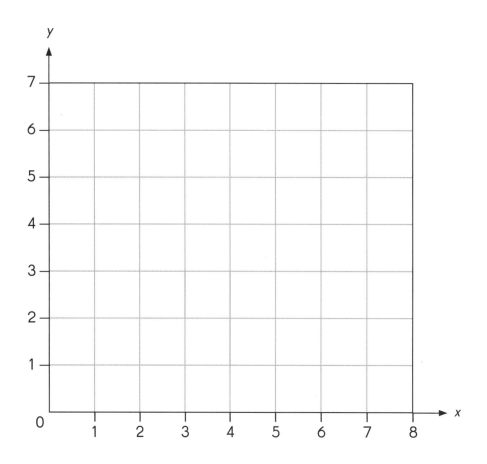

Name: _____   **Date:** _____

Use the graph to answer the questions.

The perimeter of a square is P centimeters and the length of each side is s centimeters. A graph of $P = 4s$ is drawn.

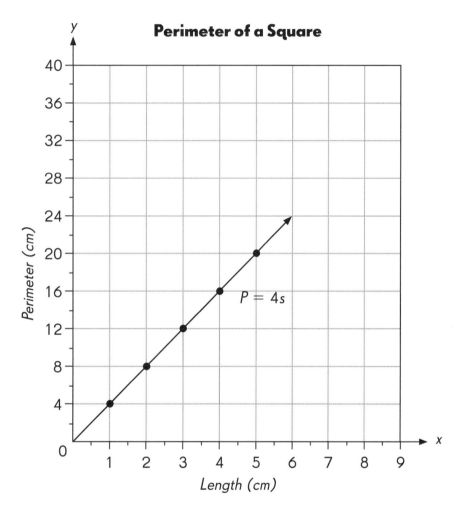

13. What is the perimeter of a square of side 2 centimeters? _____

14. What is the perimeter of a square of side 4.5 centimeters? _____

15. What is the length of a side of a square if its perimeter is 4 centimeters? _____

16. What is the length of a side of a square if its perimeter is 10 centimeters? _____

17. If the point $(7, M)$ is on the graph, what is the value of M? _____

Complete the table.

18. Each bottle contains 2 liters of cooking oil.

Number of Bottles (x)	1	2	3		5	6
Number of Liters (y)	2		6	8		12

Complete the graph using the data in the table. Then answer the questions.

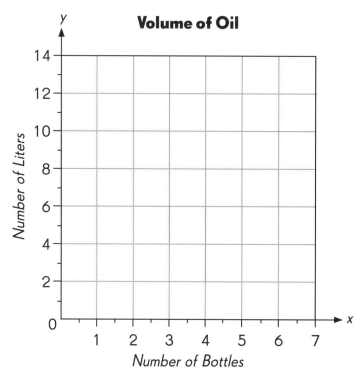

19. How many liters of oil are in 3 bottles? _____

20. How many liters of oil are in 2.5 bottles? _____

21. How many bottles contain 8 liters of oil? _____

22. How many bottles contain 7 liters of oil? _____

23. How many bottles contain 11 liters of oil? _____

Practice 4   Comparing Data Using Line Graphs

Complete the tables and graphs. Then answer the questions.

James walks at a pace of 20 steps per minute, and Kaylee walks at a pace of 25 steps per minute.

1.   Complete the tables.

James' Pace ($y = 20x$)

Travel Time (min)	0	1	2	3	4	5
Number of Steps	0	20				

Kaylee's Pace ($y = 25x$)

Travel Time (min)	0	1	2	3	4	5
Number of Steps	0	25				

2.   **a.**   Write the ordered pairs that represent the number of steps that James and Kaylee each takes.

b. Plot the points on a graph and join the points with two straight lines. Plot one line for James and another for Kaylee.

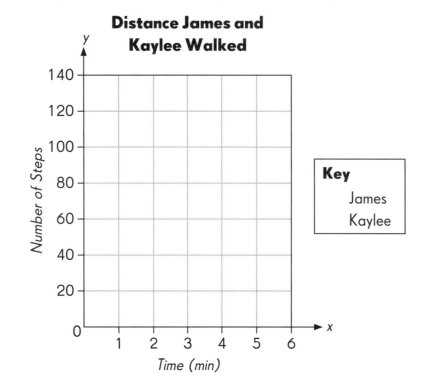

3. How many steps does each person take in 4 minutes?

4. How long does it take for each person to walk 100 steps?

5. How does the number of steps that Kaylee takes compare to the number of steps that James takes in the same amount of time?

Complete the tables and graphs. Then answer the questions.

Printer A can print 20 pages per minute. Printer B can print 30 pages per minute.

6. Complete the tables.

Printer A ($y = 20x$)

Time (min)	1	2	3	4	5
Number of Pages	20				

Printer B ($y = 30x$)

Time (min)	1	2	3	4	5
Number of Pages	30				

7. **a.** Write the ordered pairs represented by each table.

b. Plot the points on a graph. Draw a straight line joining the points for each printer.

**Pages Printed by
Two Printers**

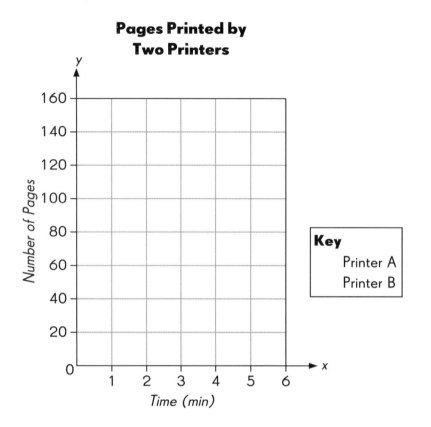

8. Which printer prints the most pages in 4 minutes? How many more?

9. Using both printers, how many pages are printed after 3 minutes?

10. How long will it take for both printers together to print 225 pages?

11. Suppose you made a graph of the number of pages that the two printers can print when running at the same time. Would this line graph be above the first two, between them, or under both of them? Explain.

Study the graph. Then answer the questions on page 118.

Two taps P and Q are turned on. Water is flowing from both of them into one container. Water from tap P flows at the rate of 60 milliliters per second. Water from tap Q flows at the rate of 30 milliliters per second.

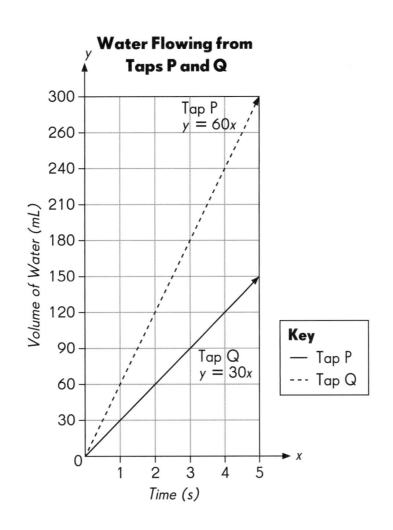

12. How much water is in the container after 3 seconds?

13. If only one tap works at a time, how long does each tap take to bring the water level up to 120 milliliters?

14. How much water will flow from each tap after 6 minutes?

15. Which tap will fill a container faster? How much faster?

Practice 5   Combinations

Complete.

A bag has 1 red, 1 blue, and 1 green marble. Another bag has 1 red and 1 blue cube.

1.   List all the possible combinations of choosing 1 marble and 1 cube.

Color of Marble	Color of Cube

2.   There are _____ combinations.

Complete.

Two leagues are competing in a soccer tournament. Each league has three teams.
Teams A, B, and C are in East League. Teams X, Y, and Z are in West League.
Each team in East League plays against every team in West League.

3.   Complete the table for the games played.

		East League		
		A	**B**	**C**
West League	**X**			
	Y			
	Z			

4.   The number of combinations of games for the six teams is _____.

Draw a tree diagram to find the number of combinations.

5. Ms. Li has 4 different books and 1 red pen, 1 blue pen, and 1 black pen.
She is wrapping one book and one pen to give as a gift.
Draw a tree diagram to find the number of combinations she can choose.

There are _____ combinations.

Find the number of combinations.

6.   Rina has 1 black, 1 red, and 1 yellow skirt.
        She has 1 white, 1 floral, and 1 striped shirt.

   a.   Draw a tree diagram to show the possible outfits Rina can wear.

   b.   Find the number of outfits by multiplication.

        The number of outfits is _____.

Complete.

7. There are 4 colors on a spinner. There are 6 faces on a number cube, numbered 1 to 6. The spinner is spun and the number cube is tossed.

There are _____ combinations of color and number.

8. A bookshelf has 10 mathematics books, 8 science books, and 12 history books.

a. There are _____ combinations of a mathematics book and a science book.

b. There are _____ combinations of a science book and a history book.

c. There are _____ combinations of a mathematics book and a history book.

Practice 6   Theoretical Probability and Experimental Probability

Use the table to answer the questions. Express each probability as a decimal.

A spinner has four equal sections in four different colors, red, blue, green, and yellow. The spinner is spun 100 times. The table shows the number of times it lands on each color.

Outcome	Number of Times
lands on red	28
lands on blue	25
lands on green	24
lands on yellow	23

1. What is the experimental probability of landing on red?

_____

2. What is the experimental probability of landing on blue?

_____

3. What is the experimental probability of landing on green?

_____

4. What is the experimental probability of landing on yellow?

_____

5. What is the theoretical probability of landing on each of the four colors?

_____

Use the table to answer the questions. Express each probability as a fraction in its simplest form.

A number cube has 1 face numbered 1, 2 faces numbered 2, and 3 faces numbered 3. The cube is tossed 100 times. The table shows the number of times each number is shown.

Outcome	Number of Times
cube shows 1	14
cube shows 2	34
cube shows 3	52

6. What is the experimental probability of the cube showing 1?

   _____

7. What is the theoretical probability of the cube showing 1?

   _____

8. What is the experimental probability of the cube showing 2?

   _____

9. What is the theoretical probability of the cube showing 2?

   _____

10. What is the experimental probability of the cube showing 3?

   _____

11. What is the theoretical probability of the cube showing 3?

   _____

Use the table to answer the questions. Express each probability as a decimal.

A bag contains 2 blue marbles, 3 red marbles, and 5 green marbles.
A marble is drawn from the bag, its color is noted and the marble is returned
to the bag. The table shows the results of drawing a marble 200 times.

Outcome	Number of Times
blue marble	36
red marble	56
green marble	108

12. What is the experimental probability of drawing a blue marble?

_____

13. What is the theoretical probability of drawing a blue marble?

_____

14. What is the experimental probability of drawing a red marble?

_____

15. What is the theoretical probability of drawing a red marble?

_____

16. What is the experimental probability of drawing a green marble?

_____

17. What is the theoretical probability of drawing a green marble?

_____

Complete.

A spinner is divided into 16 equal parts. Each part is colored green, yellow, or blue. The spinner is spun 25 times. The tally chart shows the number of times it lands on each color.

Color	Tally	Number
green	////	4
yellow	HHT ////	9
blue	HHT HHT //	12

18. Which is the likely set of colors on the spinner, Set A, Set B, or Set C?

   Set _____

	Green	Yellow	Blue
Set A	3	10	3
Set B	6	5	5
Set C	2	6	8

19. What is the experimental probability of landing on green?

   _____

20. What is the experimental probability of landing on yellow?

   _____

21. What is the experimental probability of landing on blue?

   _____

Put On Your Thinking Cap!

Challenging Practice

Complete.

1.   The table shows the conversion from gallons to pints. Complete the table.

Number of Gallons (x)	1	2	3	4	5	6
Number of Pints (y)		16			40	

2.   Write the equation relating the number of pints (y) to the number of gallons (x).

_____

3.   Draw the graph of the equation. Label the axes and the equation.

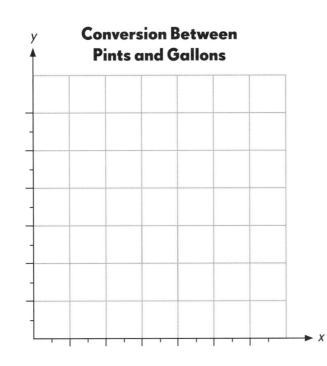

Conversion Between Pints and Gallons

Use the graph to answer the questions.

4. How many pints is $3\frac{1}{2}$ gallons?

5. How many pints is $4\frac{1}{2}$ gallons?

6. How many gallons is 20 pints?

7. How many gallons is 44 pints?

Complete.

8. The table shows the conversion from quarts to cups. Complete the table.

Number of Quarts (x)	1	2	3			6
Number of Cups (y)		8		16	20	24

9. Write the equation relating the number of cups (y) to the number of quarts (x).

_____

Put On Your Thinking Cap!

Problem Solving

Solve.

1. Jim has a dime, a nickel, and a quarter. How many different amounts of money can he form using one or more of these coins?

2. There are an equal number of red, blue, and green beads in a bag.
One bead is picked, its color is noted and the bead is replaced.
Then a second bead is picked.

a. Draw a tree diagram to show the outcomes.

b. What is the probability of picking two red beads? _____

c. What is the probability of picking one red and one green bead?

_____

d. What is the probability of picking no red beads? _____

Angles

Practice 1   Angles on a Line

In each figure, $\overleftrightarrow{AC}$ is a line. Use a protractor to find the unknown angle measures.

1.

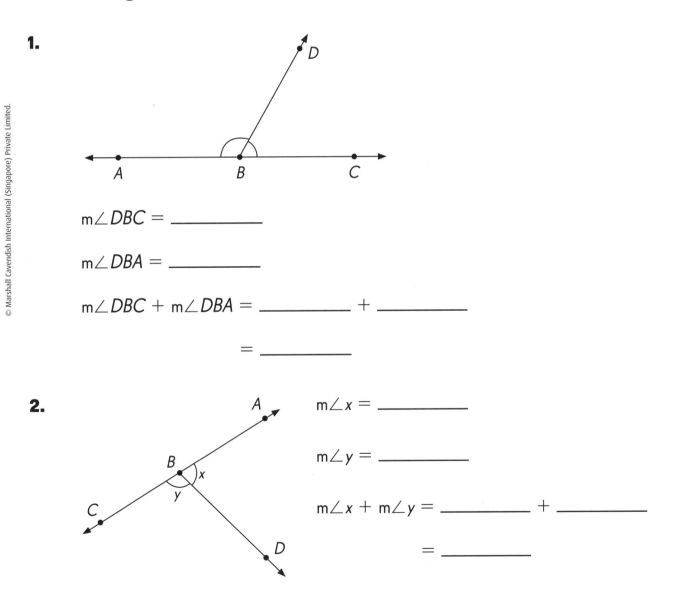

$m\angle DBC = $ _____

$m\angle DBA = $ _____

$m\angle DBC + m\angle DBA = $ _____ + _____

$= $ _____

2.

$m\angle x = $ _____

$m\angle y = $ _____

$m\angle x + m\angle y = $ _____ + _____

$= $ _____

$\overleftrightarrow{AC}$ is a line. Use a protractor to find the unknown
angle measures.

3.

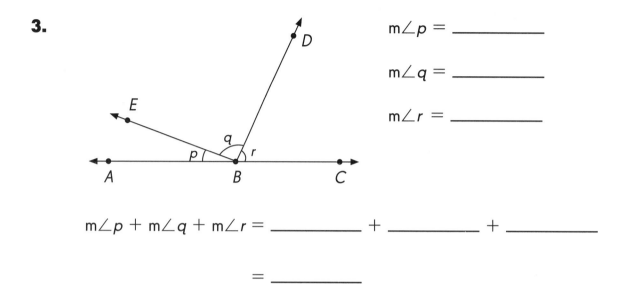

m∠p = _____

m∠q = _____

m∠r = _____

m∠p + m∠q + m∠r = _____ + _____ + _____

= _____

Name the angles on each line.

4. $\overleftrightarrow{XZ}$ is a line.

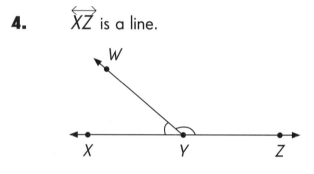

_____

5. $\overleftrightarrow{PR}$ is a line.

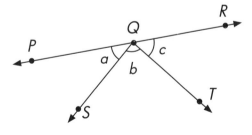

_____

Name each set of angles on a line.

6. $\overleftrightarrow{AC}$ is a line.

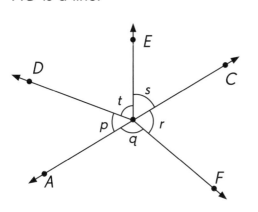

_____

_____

7. $\overleftrightarrow{AB}$ and $\overleftrightarrow{CD}$ are lines.

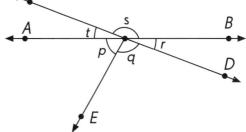

_____

_____

_____

Find the unknown angle measures.

8. $\overleftrightarrow{AC}$ is a line. Find the measure of $\angle DBC$.

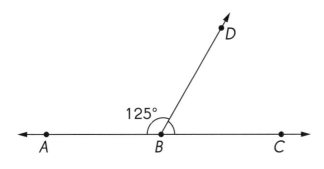

m$\angle DBC$ + 125° = 180°

m$\angle DBC$ = 180° − _____

= _____

9. $\overleftrightarrow{EG}$ is a line. Find the measure of $\angle HFE$.

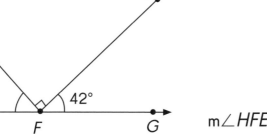

m$\angle HFE$ = _____

Find the unknown angle measures.

10. $\overleftrightarrow{OQ}$ is a line. Find the measure of $\angle SPT$.

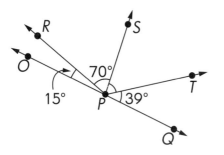

m$\angle SPT =$ _____

11. $\overleftrightarrow{AC}$ is a line. Find the measure of $\angle EBF$.

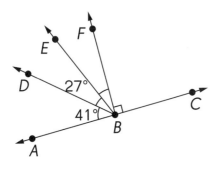

m$\angle EBF =$ _____

12. $\overleftrightarrow{JK}$ is a line. Find the measures of $\angle y$ and $\angle z$.

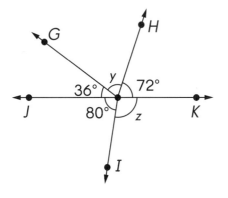

m$\angle y =$ _____

m$\angle z =$ _____

13. $\overleftrightarrow{EF}$ and $\overleftrightarrow{GH}$ are lines. Find the measures of $\angle a$ and $\angle b$.

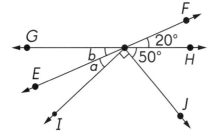

m$\angle a =$ _____

m$\angle b =$ _____

Practice 2   Angles at a Point

In each figure, the rays meet at a point. Use a protractor to find unknown angle measures.

1.

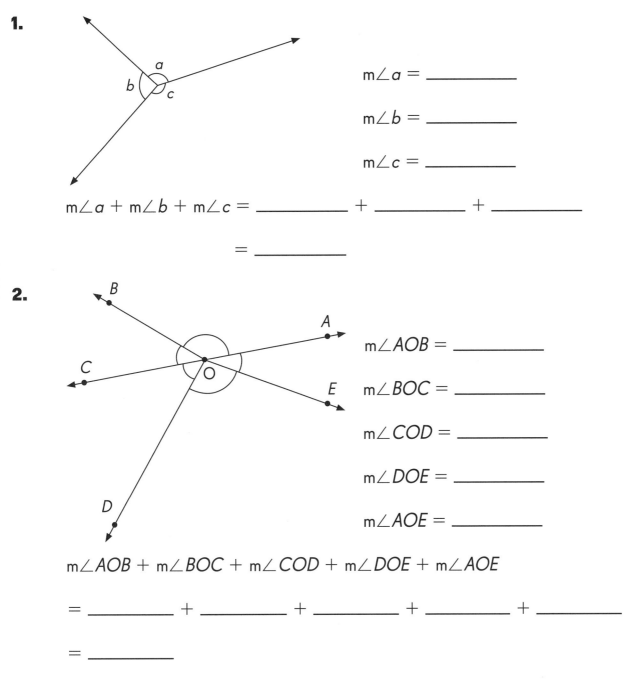

$m\angle a =$ _____

$m\angle b =$ _____

$m\angle c =$ _____

$m\angle a + m\angle b + m\angle c =$ _____ + _____ + _____

= _____

2.

$m\angle AOB =$ _____

$m\angle BOC =$ _____

$m\angle COD =$ _____

$m\angle DOE =$ _____

$m\angle AOE =$ _____

$m\angle AOB + m\angle BOC + m\angle COD + m\angle DOE + m\angle AOE$

= _____ + _____ + _____ + _____ + _____

= _____

Name the angles at a point.

3.

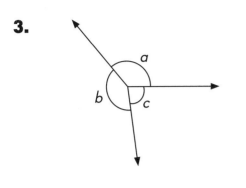

_____

4.

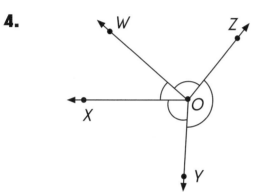

_____

5.

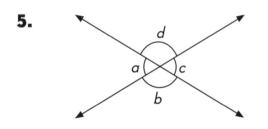

_____

6.

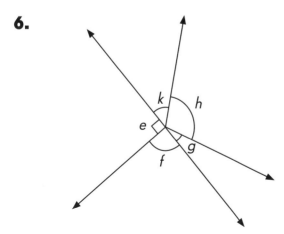

_____

Find the unknown angle measures.

7.   Find the measure of ∠AOB.

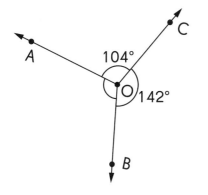

m∠AOB = _____

8.   Find the measure of ∠a.

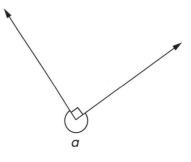

m∠a = _____

9.   Find the measure of ∠b.

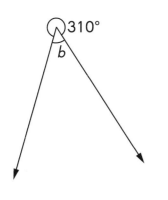

m∠b = _____

10.   Find the measure of ∠c.

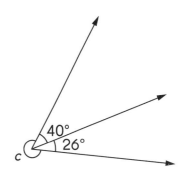

m∠c = _____

Find the unknown angle measures.

11. Find the measure of ∠q.

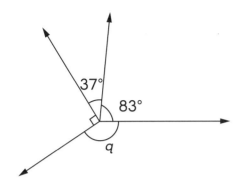

m∠q = _____

12. Find the measure of ∠r.

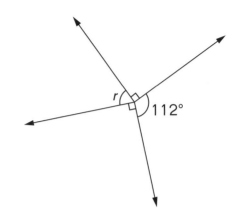

m∠r = _____

13. Find the measure of ∠a.

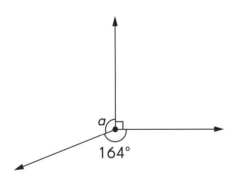

m∠a = _____

14. $\overleftrightarrow{PR}$ and $\overleftrightarrow{TU}$ meet at Q. Find the measures of ∠PQS and ∠TQR.

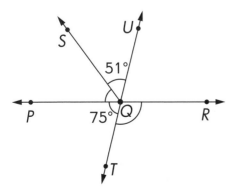

m∠PQS = _____

m∠TQR = _____

Practice 3   Vertical Angles

Complete.

1. $\overleftrightarrow{AB}$ and $\overleftrightarrow{CD}$ meet at O. Use a protractor to find unknown angle measures.

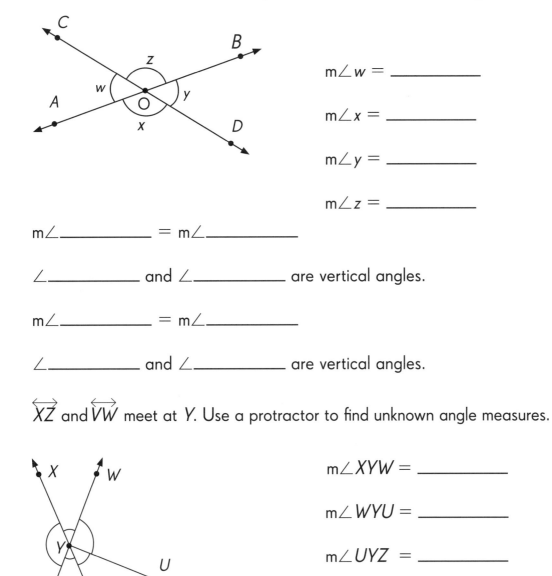

m∠w = _____

m∠x = _____

m∠y = _____

m∠z = _____

m∠_____ = m∠_____

∠_____ and ∠_____ are vertical angles.

m∠_____ = m∠_____

∠_____ and ∠_____ are vertical angles.

2. $\overleftrightarrow{XZ}$ and $\overleftrightarrow{VW}$ meet at Y. Use a protractor to find unknown angle measures.

m∠XYW = _____

m∠WYU = _____

m∠UYZ = _____

m∠ZYV = _____

m∠VYX = _____

∠_____ and ∠_____ are vertical angles.

∠_____ and ∠_____ are vertical angles.

Complete.

3. Look at the star and its marked angles. In the table below, write three sets of
   a. angles on a line,
   b. angles at a point,
   c. vertical angles.

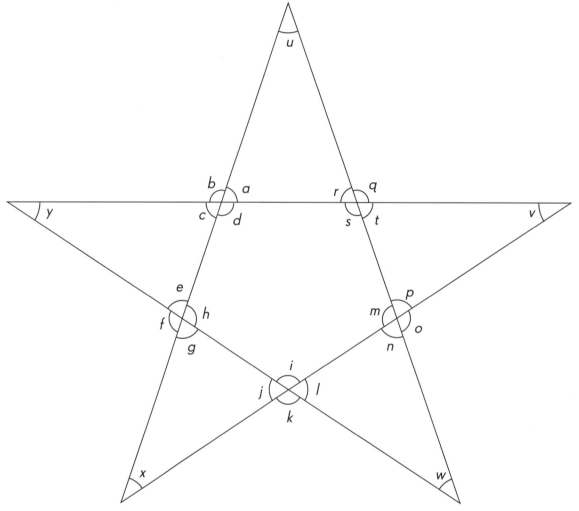

Angles on a Line	Angles at a Point	Vertical Angles
∠b and ∠c	∠a, ∠b, ∠c, and ∠d	∠a and ∠c

Draw.

4.   Draw rays at P to form
   a.   an angle whose measure forms a sum of 180° with the measure of $\angle x$,
   b.   an angle whose measure is equal to the measure of $\angle x$.
   (Do not use a protractor to draw the angles.)

a.

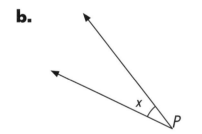

b.

Find the unknown angle measures.

5. $\overleftrightarrow{AB}$ and $\overleftrightarrow{CD}$ meet at O. Find the measure of $\angle COB$.

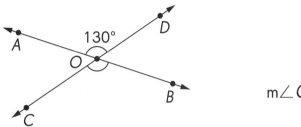

$m\angle COB =$ _____

6. $\overleftrightarrow{EF}$ and $\overleftrightarrow{GH}$ meet at O. Find the measures of $\angle GOF$ and $\angle EOH$.

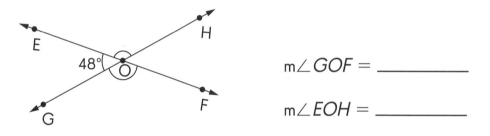

$m\angle GOF =$ _____

$m\angle EOH =$ _____

7. $\overleftrightarrow{RS}$ and $\overleftrightarrow{PQ}$ meet at N. Find the measures of $\angle PNR$, $\angle RNQ$, and $\angle QNS$.

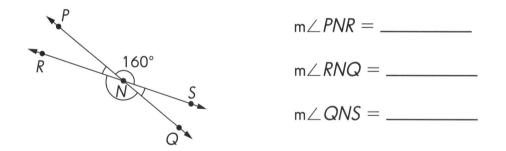

$m\angle PNR =$ _____

$m\angle RNQ =$ _____

$m\angle QNS =$ _____

Find the unknown angle measures.

8. $\overleftrightarrow{JK}$ and $\overleftrightarrow{LM}$ meet at O. Find the measure of ∠NOK.

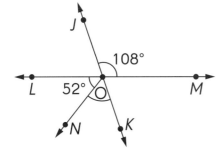

m∠NOK = _____

9. $\overleftrightarrow{AB}$, $\overleftrightarrow{CD}$, and $\overleftrightarrow{EF}$ meet at O. Find the measure of ∠x.

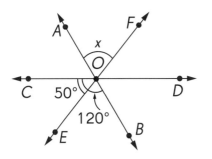

m∠x = _____

10. $\overleftrightarrow{AB}$ and $\overleftrightarrow{CD}$ meet at O. Find the measure of ∠w.

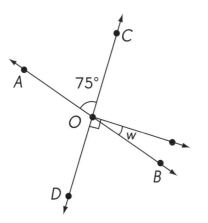

m∠w = _____

Find the unknown angle measures.

11. $\overleftrightarrow{QR}$ and $\overleftrightarrow{ST}$ meet at O. Find the measures of $\angle QOS$, $\angle TOR$, and $\angle SOR$.

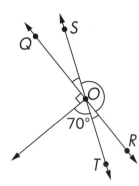

m$\angle QOS =$ _____

m$\angle TOR =$ _____

m$\angle SOR =$ _____

12. $\overleftrightarrow{AB}$ and $\overleftrightarrow{CD}$ meet at O. Find the measures of $\angle p$, $\angle q$, and $\angle r$.

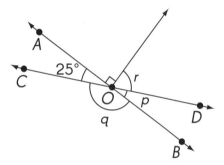

m$\angle p =$ _____

m$\angle q =$ _____

m$\angle r =$ _____

13. $\overleftrightarrow{UV}$, $\overleftrightarrow{WX}$, and $\overleftrightarrow{YZ}$ meet at O. Find the measure of $\angle UOW$.

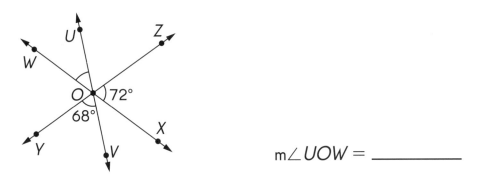

m$\angle UOW =$ _____

14. $\overleftrightarrow{AB}$, $\overleftrightarrow{CD}$, and $\overleftrightarrow{EF}$ meet at O. Find the measures of $\angle x$ and $\angle y$.

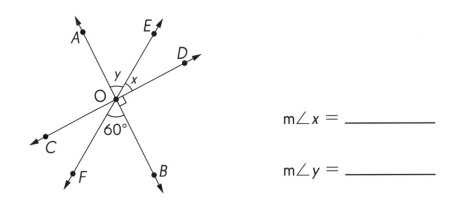

m$\angle x =$ _____

m$\angle y =$ _____

Math Journal

Check the box for each correct statement.
Then explain your answer.

1. $\overleftrightarrow{XY}$ is a line.

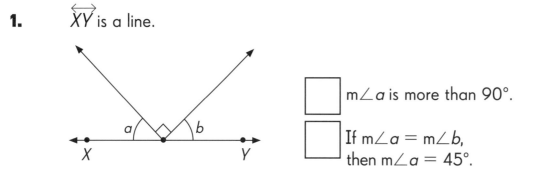

$\square$ $m\angle a$ is more than 90°.

$\square$ If $m\angle a = m\angle b$,
then $m\angle a = 45°$.

2. $\overleftrightarrow{AB}$ and $\overleftrightarrow{CD}$ meet at O.

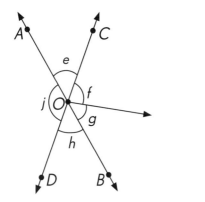

$\square$ $m\angle e = m\angle h$

$\square$ $m\angle f + m\angle g = m\angle j$

$\square$ $m\angle e = m\angle g$

Put On Your Thinking Cap!

Challenging Practice

Find the unknown angle measures. Explain.

1. $\overleftrightarrow{GJ}$ is a line. $\angle LHK$ is a right angle. Find the measure of $\angle LHJ$.

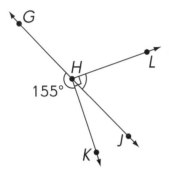

2. $\overleftrightarrow{MN}$ and $\overleftrightarrow{XY}$ meet at O and $m\angle a = m\angle b$.
   Find the measure of $\angle c$.

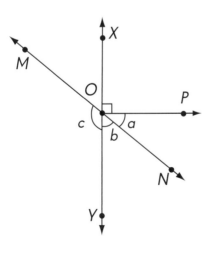

3. $\overleftrightarrow{AC}$ is a line. $\angle ABE$ and $\angle DBF$ are right angles.
Find the measure of $\angle FBC$.

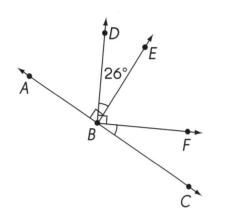

4. $\overleftrightarrow{AB}$ and $\overleftrightarrow{WX}$ meet at O. $\angle COB$ and $\angle YOX$ are right angles.
Find the measures of $\angle AOX$ and $\angle COY$.

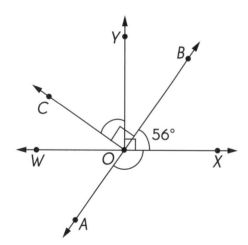

Put On Your Thinking Cap!

Problem Solving

Solve.

1. $\overleftrightarrow{JK}$ and $\overleftrightarrow{LM}$ are lines.
Check the box for each correct statement.

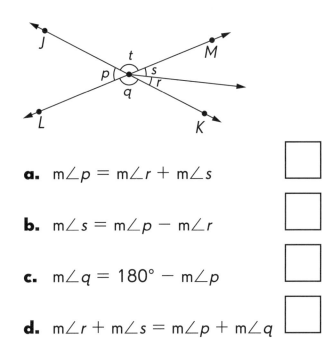

a. $m\angle p = m\angle r + m\angle s$ ☐

b. $m\angle s = m\angle p - m\angle r$ ☐

c. $m\angle q = 180° - m\angle p$ ☐

d. $m\angle r + m\angle s = m\angle p + m\angle q$ ☐

2. $\overleftrightarrow{AB}$, $\overleftrightarrow{CD}$, and $\overleftrightarrow{EF}$ meet at O. Find the sum of the measures of $\angle AOC$, $\angle FOD$, and $\angle BOE$.

$m\angle AOC + m\angle FOD + m\angle BOE = $ _____

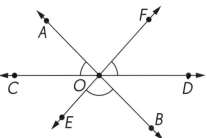

3. ABCD is a square. $\overrightarrow{BE}$ is a ray. Find the measure of $\angle x$.

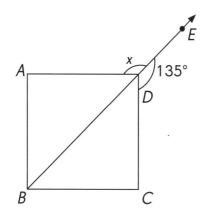

4. How many degrees does the hour hand of a clock turn between 3 P.M. and 7:30 P.M.?

5. $\overleftrightarrow{AB}$ is a line. The measures of $\angle a$ and $\angle b$ are whole numbers.

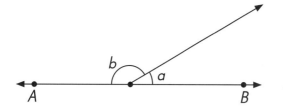

If the measure of $\angle b$ is twice that of $\angle a$, find the measures of $\angle a$ and $\angle b$.

for Chapters 11 and 12

Concepts and Skills

Make a line plot using the data. Then answer the questions. *(Lesson 11.1)*

The table shows the capacity of some bottles.

Capacity of Bottles (L)	$\frac{1}{2}$	$\frac{5}{8}$	$\frac{3}{4}$	1
Number of Bottles	2	4	2	3

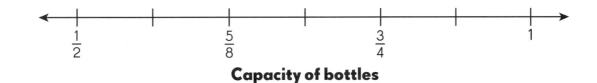

Capacity of bottles

1. How many bottles are there in all? _____

2. What is the difference between the capacity of a $\frac{3}{4}$-liter bottle and a

$\frac{5}{8}$-liter bottle? _____

3. What is the total capacity of all the bottles? _____

Use the data in the graph below to answer the questions. *(Lesson 11.2)*

The double bar graph shows the number of pairs of black jeans and blue jeans produced in a factory in three days.

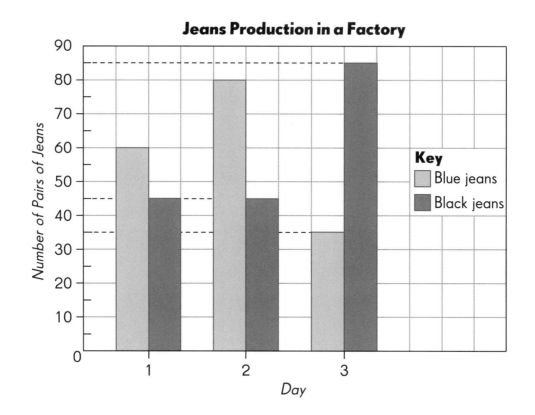

Jeans Production in a Factory

Key
■ Blue jeans
■ Black jeans

Number of Pairs of Jeans

Day

4. On day 2, _____ more pairs of blue jeans than black jeans are produced.

5. On day _____ and day _____ , the same number of pairs of black jeans are produced.

6. The greatest number of blue jeans is produced on day _____.

7. On day 1, the difference between the number of pairs of blue jeans and black jeans produced is _____.

8. The total number of pairs of jeans produced in the three days is _____.

9. The ratio of the number of pairs of black jeans produced to the number of pairs of blue jeans produced on day 3 is _____.

10. Express the number of black jeans produced on day 1 as a fraction of the number of blue jeans produced on day 1. _____

11. Express the total number of blue jeans produced as a percent of the total number of jeans produced in the three days. _____

Complete the graph using the data in the table. *(Lesson 11.3)*

Quarts of Milk	1	2	3	4
Cups of Milk	4	8	12	16

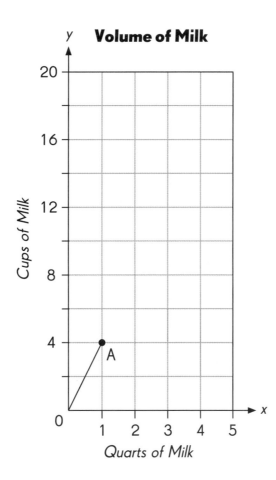

Use the graph on page 153 to answer the questions. *(Lesson 11.3)*

12. What are the coordinates of point *A*? _____

13. How many quarts of milk are in 12 cups? _____

14. How many cups of milk are in $3\frac{1}{2}$ quarts of milk? _____

15. How many cups of milk are in 5 quarts of milk? _____

Complete. *(Lesson 11.4)*

Peter's toy car runs at 20 meters per minute and Steve's toy car runs at 15 meters per minute. Complete the two tables that show the total distance the two toy cars traveled in 4 minutes.

16. Complete the tables.

Peter's Toy Car

Travel Time (min)	0	1	2	3	4
Total Distance (m)	0	20			

Steve's Toy Car

Travel Time (min)	0	1	2	3	4
Total Distance (m)	0	15			

17.   Plot the points of each graph on a coordinate grid.

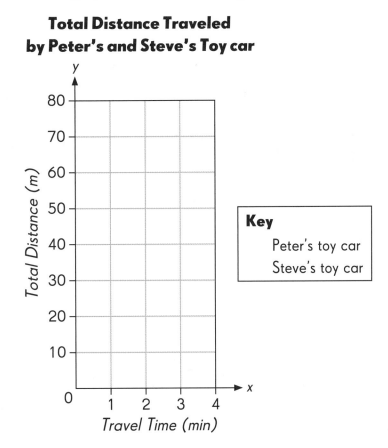

**Total Distance Traveled
by Peter's and Steve's Toy car**

Use the graphs above to answer the questions.

18.   How far does each car travel in 3 minutes?

19.   How long does each car take to travel 60 meters?

20.   How far does each car travel after 5 minutes?

Make an organized list to find the number of combinations. *(Lesson 11.5)*

Barry's Yogurt Shop sells frozen yogurt with a topping. A customer can pick one of three flavors: vanilla, strawberry, and blueberry. The customer can pick one of three toppings: nuts, raisins, and sprinkles.

21. List all the possible combinations of yogurt flavor and topping.

Yogurt Flavor	Topping

22. There are _____ combinations.

Find the number of combinations. *(Lesson 11.5)*

Brenda has 1 red, 1 green, and 1 gold bracelet. She has 4 pairs of earrings:
stud, hoop, button, and dangling. She wants to find all the combinations of
1 bracelet and 1 pair of earrings that she can wear.

23. Draw a tree diagram to show the possible combinations.

24. Find the number of combinations by multiplication.

There are _____ combinations.

Complete. *(Lesson 11.6)*

A bag has 5 green toothbrushes and 7 yellow toothbrushes. Tim and Cathy each pick a toothbrush, and then return it to the bag. They do this for 20 times each. The table shows some of their results.

25. Complete the table.

	Number of Times a Green Toothbrush Is Picked	Number of Times a Yellow Toothbrush Is Picked	Probability of Picking a Green Toothbrush	Probability of Picking a Yellow Toothbrush
Tim	12			
Cathy		9		

26. The theoretical probability of picking a yellow toothbrush is _____.

27. The experimental probability of picking a green toothbrush that Tim's results

show is _____.

Find the unknown angle measures. *(Lesson 12.1)*

28. $\overleftrightarrow{AB}$ is a line.

29. $\overleftrightarrow{AB}$ is a line. The measures of $\angle a$, $\angle b$, and $\angle c$ are equal.

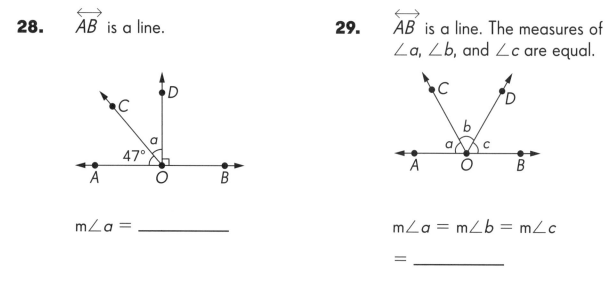

$m\angle a =$ _____

$m\angle a = m\angle b = m\angle c$

$=$ _____

Find the unknown angle measures. *(Lessons 12.1 and 12.2)*

30. $\overleftrightarrow{AB}$ is a line.

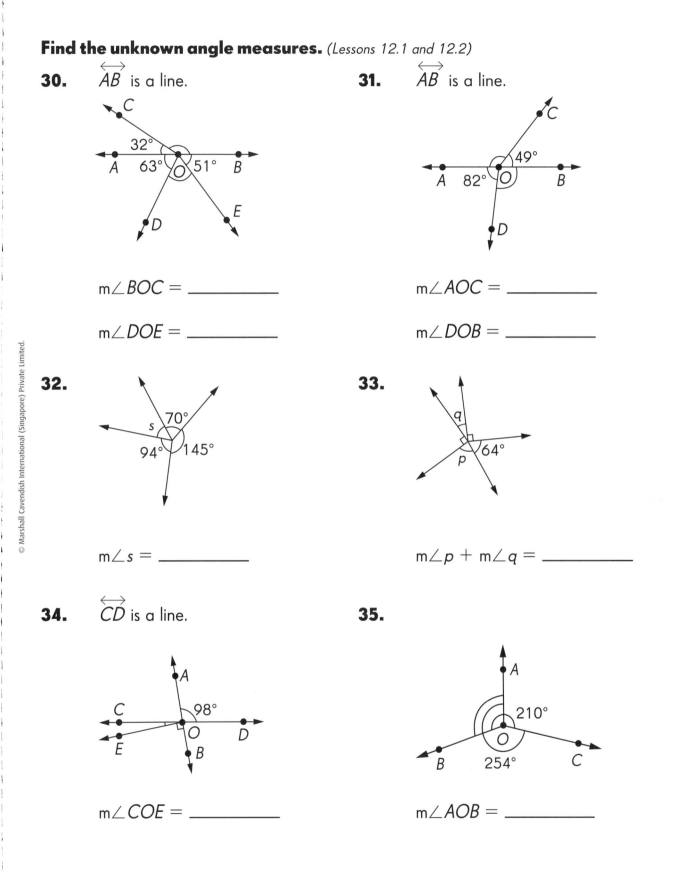

m∠BOC = _____

m∠DOE = _____

31. $\overleftrightarrow{AB}$ is a line.

m∠AOC = _____

m∠DOB = _____

32.

m∠s = _____

33.

m∠p + m∠q = _____

34. $\overleftrightarrow{CD}$ is a line.

m∠COE = _____

35.

m∠AOB = _____

Find the unknown angle measures. *(Lesson 12.3)*

$\overleftrightarrow{AB}$, $\overleftrightarrow{CD}$, and $\overleftrightarrow{EF}$ are lines.

36.

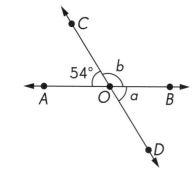

m∠a = _____

m∠b = _____

37.

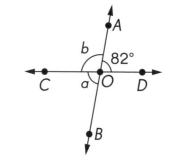

m∠a = _____

m∠b = _____

38.

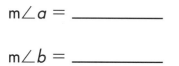
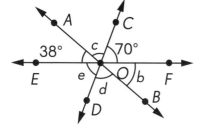

m∠b = _____

m∠c = _____

m∠d = _____

m∠e = _____

m∠b + m∠d + m∠e

= _____

39.

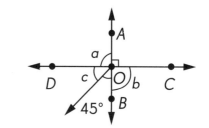

m∠a = _____

m∠b = _____

m∠c = _____

Problem Solving

Solve. Show your work.

The graph shows a measurement in yards (*x*-axis) and its corresponding measurement in feet (*y*-axis).

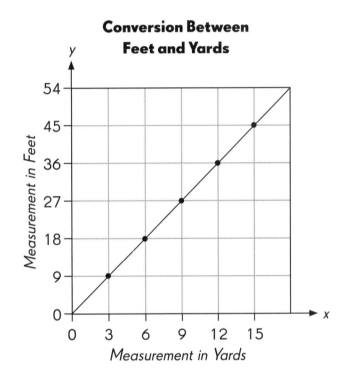

Conversion Between Feet and Yards

40. The cost of 3 yards of fabric is $24. What is the cost of 36 feet of fabric?

Solve. Show your work.

41. Each letter of the word JOURNAL is written on separate cards and put into a bag. First, one card is drawn. Then, the card is colored blue or yellow.

   a. Draw a tree diagram to show the possible combinations of cards and colors.

   b. What is the theoretical probability of picking a combination with a vowel?

© Marshall Cavendish International (Singapore) Private Limited.

Chapter 13 Properties of Triangles and Four-Sided Figures

Practice 1 Classifying Triangles

**Which of these triangles are equilateral, isosceles, or scalene?
Use a centimeter ruler to find out.**

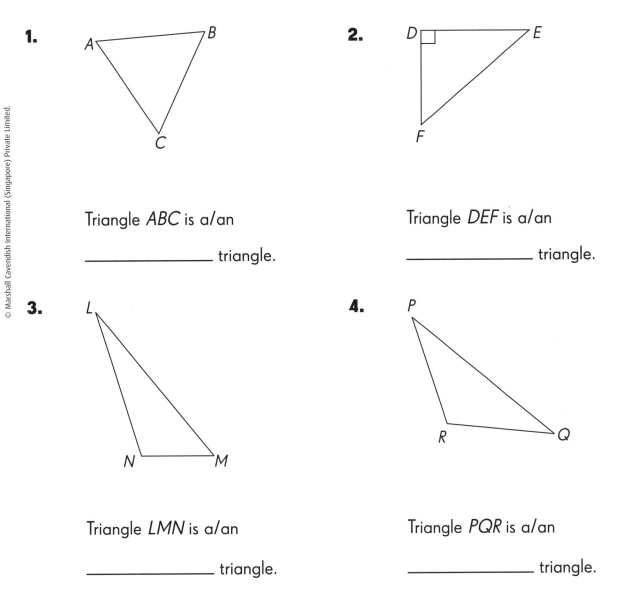

1.

Triangle *ABC* is a/an

_____ triangle.

2.

Triangle *DEF* is a/an

_____ triangle.

3.

Triangle *LMN* is a/an

_____ triangle.

4.

Triangle *PQR* is a/an

_____ triangle.

Which of these triangles are right, obtuse, or acute?
Use a protractor to find out.

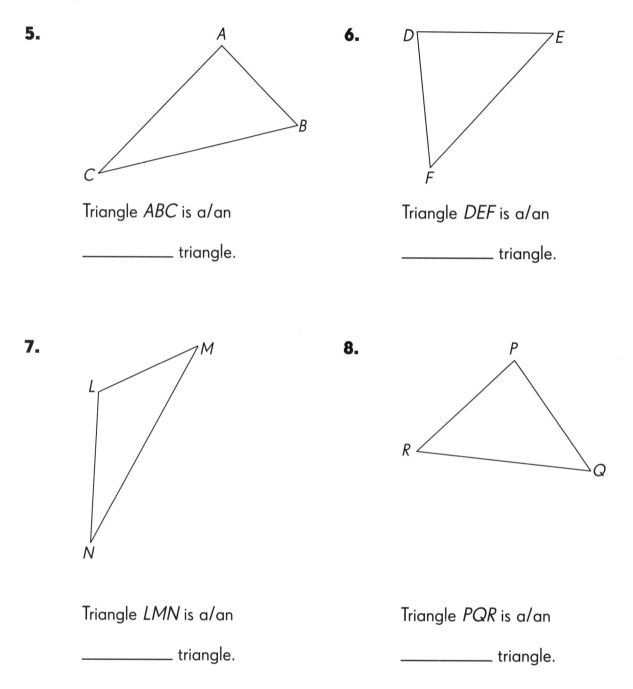

5.

Triangle *ABC* is a/an

_____ triangle.

6.

Triangle *DEF* is a/an

_____ triangle.

7.

Triangle *LMN* is a/an

_____ triangle.

8.

Triangle *PQR* is a/an

_____ triangle.

Practice 2   Measures of Angles of a Triangle

Complete.

1.

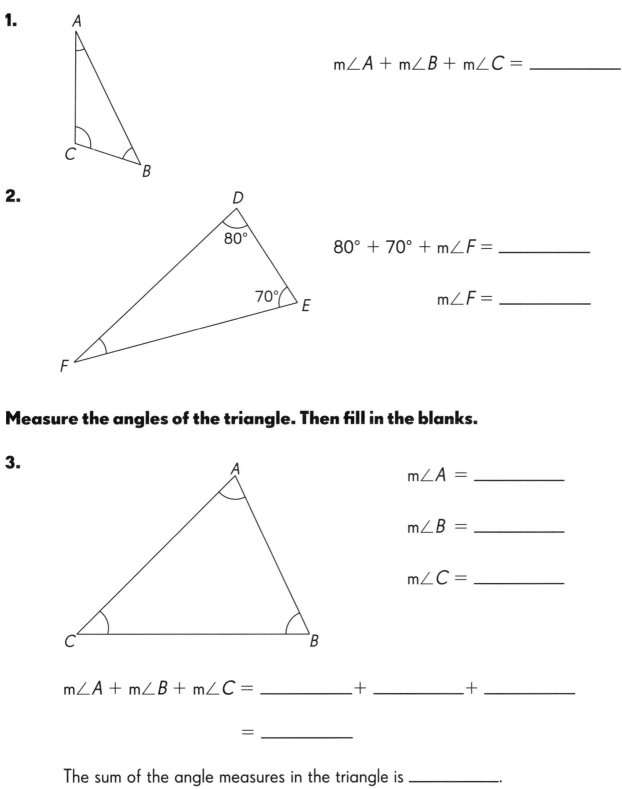

$m\angle A + m\angle B + m\angle C =$ _____

2.

$80° + 70° + m\angle F =$ _____

$m\angle F =$ _____

Measure the angles of the triangle. Then fill in the blanks.

3.

$m\angle A =$ _____

$m\angle B =$ _____

$m\angle C =$ _____

$m\angle A + m\angle B + m\angle C =$ _____ + _____ + _____

$=$ _____

The sum of the angle measures in the triangle is _____.

These triangles are not drawn to scale. Find the unknown angle measures.

4. Find the measure of ∠B.

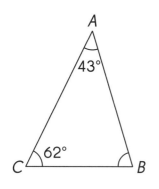

5. Find the measure of ∠D.

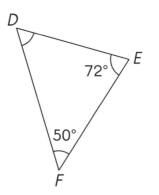

6. Find the measure of ∠H.

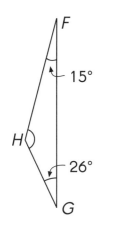

7. Find the measure of ∠QPS.

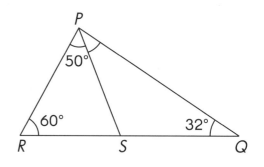

Practice 3 Right, Isosceles, and Equilateral Triangles

Complete. *ABC* and *EFG* are right triangles.

1.

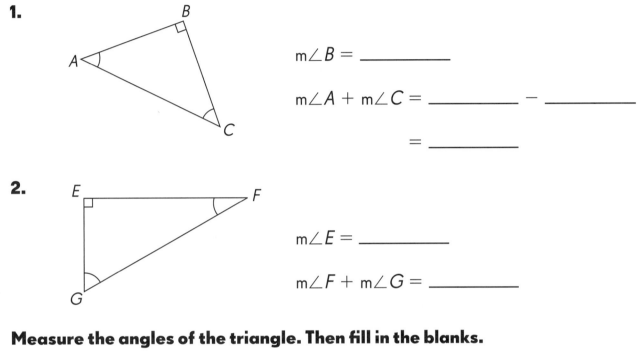

$m\angle B = $ _____

$m\angle A + m\angle C = $ _____ − _____

$= $ _____

2.

$m\angle E = $ _____

$m\angle F + m\angle G = $ _____

Measure the angles of the triangle. Then fill in the blanks.

3.

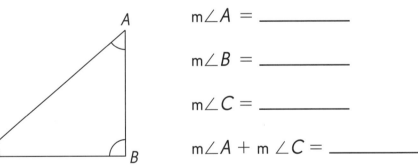

$m\angle A = $ _____

$m\angle B = $ _____

$m\angle C = $ _____

$m\angle A + m\angle C = $ _____

These triangles are not drawn to scale. Identify and shade the right triangles.

4.

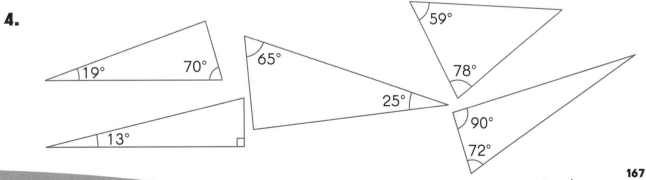

19°   70°

13°

65°

25°

59°

78°

90°

72°

These triangles are not drawn to scale. Find the unknown angle measures.

5.   Find the sum of the measures of ∠A and ∠B.

6.   Find the measure of ∠C.

7.   Find the measures of ∠ADC and ∠ABC.

8.   Find the measures of ∠EGF and ∠DGE.

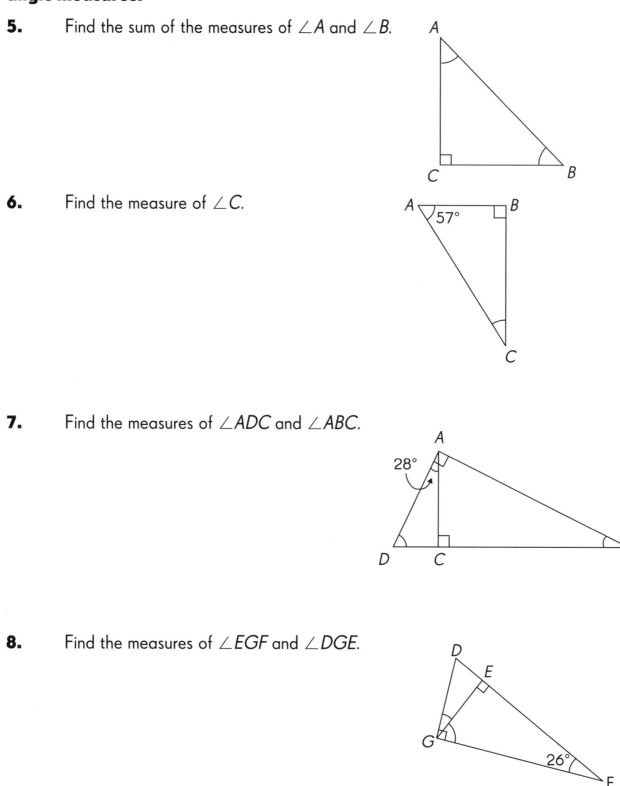

Complete. *XYZ* and *PQR* are isosceles triangles.

9.

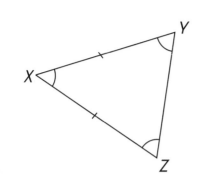

Which two sides are of equal length?

_____

Which two angles have equal measures?

_____

10.

Which two sides are of equal length?

_____

Which two angles have equal measures?

_____

**These triangles are not drawn to scale. Identify and shade
the isosceles triangles.**

11.

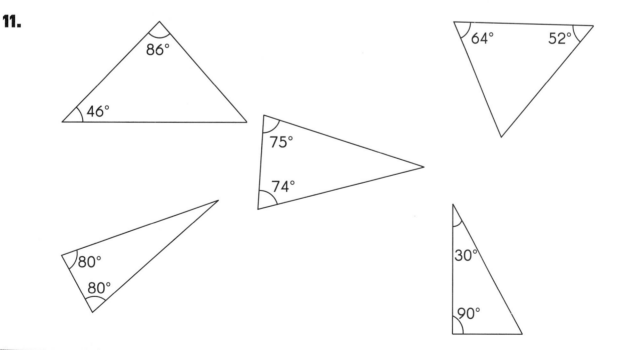

These triangles are not drawn to scale. Find the unknown angle measures.

12. Find the measure of ∠F.

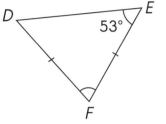

13. Find the measure of ∠C.

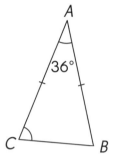

14. Find the measure of ∠TRS.

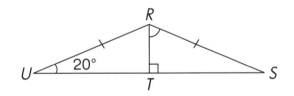

15. Find the measure of ∠d.

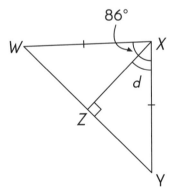

Complete. Use your protractor and centimeter ruler to measure the sides and angles. Which figure is an equilateral triangle? Check the box.

16.

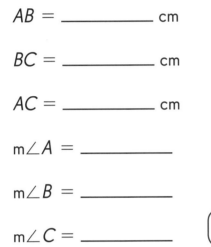

AB = _____ cm

BC = _____ cm

AC = _____ cm

m∠A = _____

m∠B = _____

m∠C = _____ ☐

17.

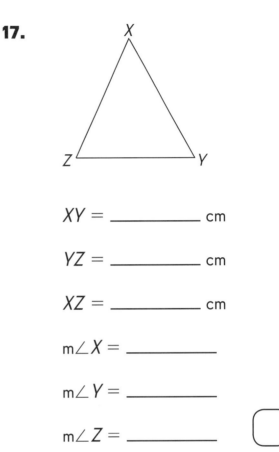

XY = _____ cm

YZ = _____ cm

XZ = _____ cm

m∠X = _____

m∠Y = _____

m∠Z = _____ ☐

Complete. *ABC* is an equilateral triangle.

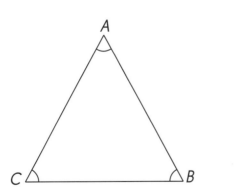

18. Which angles have measures equal to the measure of ∠A?

_____

19. Which sides have lengths equal to the length of $\overline{AB}$?

_____

20. What can you say about the angles of triangle *ABC* ?

_____

These triangles are not drawn to scale. Identify and shade the equilateral triangles.

21.

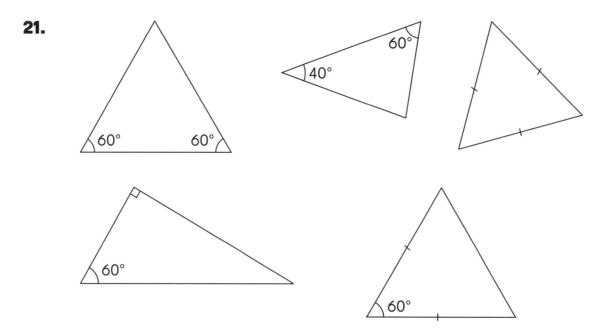

These triangles are not drawn to scale. Find the unknown angle measures.

22.   Find the measure of ∠Q.

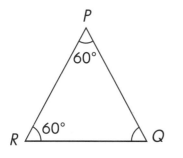

23.   Find the measures of ∠Y and ∠Z.

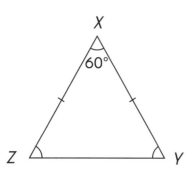

These triangles are not drawn to scale. Find the unknown angle measures.

24. $WX = XY = YW$. Find the measure of $\angle d$.

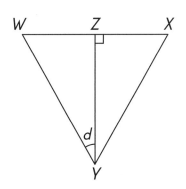

25. Find the measure of $\angle e$.

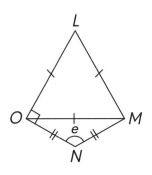

26. Triangle *PQR* is an equilateral triangle. Triangle *PST* is an isosceles triangle. The measures of $\angle a$, $\angle b$, and $\angle c$ are the same. Find the measure of $\angle d$.

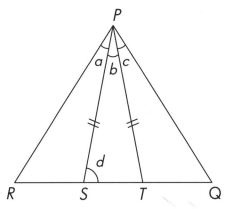

Math Journal

1. A teacher asked her students to sketch and label the angles of a triangle. These are the angle measures that three students chose to draw.

   Wayne: 120°, 80°, 10°   Ashley: 70°, 28°, 72°   Frank: 51°, 37°, 92°

   Will each student be able to draw his or her triangle? Explain your answer.

   Wayne: _____

   Ashley: _____

   Frank: _____

2. What are two ways to identify an isosceles triangle?

3. Jordan is measuring the angles of a triangle.
   He finds out that m∠A = m∠B = 60°.
   Without measuring ∠C, he says that
   triangle ABC is an equilateral triangle.

   Is he correct? Explain why.

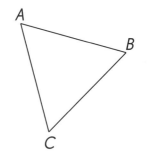

Practice 4   Triangle Inequalities

Complete. Measure the sides of the triangle to the nearest half inch. Then fill in the blanks.

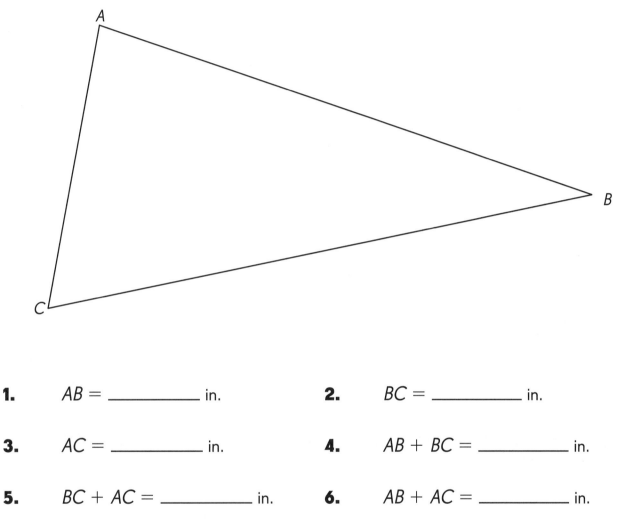

1. $AB =$ _____ in.

2. $BC =$ _____ in.

3. $AC =$ _____ in.

4. $AB + BC =$ _____ in.

5. $BC + AC =$ _____ in.

6. $AB + AC =$ _____ in.

Use your answers in Exercises 1 to 6 to answer the questions below. Fill in the blanks with *Yes* or *No*.

7.   Is $AB + BC > AC$? _____

8.   Is $BC + AC > AB$? _____

9.   Is $AB + AC > BC$? _____

Complete. Measure the sides of the triangle to the nearest centimeter. Then fill in the blanks.

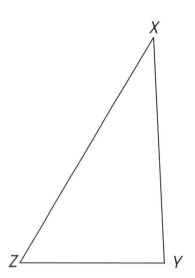

10. $XY =$ _____ cm

11. $YZ =$ _____ cm

12. $XZ =$ _____ cm

13. $XY + YZ =$ _____ cm

14. $YZ + XZ =$ _____ cm

15. $XY + XZ =$ _____ cm

Use your answers in Exercises 10 to 15 to answer the questions below. Write the sides of the triangle to make the inequalities true.

16. $XY + YZ >$ _____

17. $YZ + XZ >$ _____

18. $XY + XZ >$ _____

Name: _____   **Date:** _____

Show whether it is possible to form triangles with these lengths.

19.   6 in., 8 in., 12 in.

20.   9 in., 13 in., 3 in.

21.   2 cm, 4 cm, 7 cm

The lengths of two sides of each triangle are given. Name a possible length for the third side. The lengths are in whole centimeters or whole inches.

22.

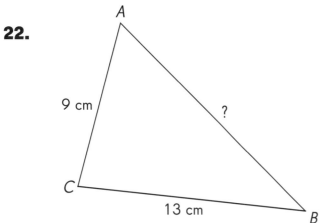

$\overline{AB}$ is greater than 10 centimeters.
A possible length for $\overline{AB}$ is

_____ centimeters.

23.

$\overline{QR}$ is greater than 9 inches.
A possible length for $\overline{QR}$ is

_____ inches.

Solve.

24. In the triangle EFG, $EF = 21$ centimeters, $FG = 11$ centimeters. The length of $\overline{EG}$ is in whole centimeters and is greater than 25 centimeters. What is a possible length of $\overline{EG}$?

© Marshall Cavendish International (Singapore) Private Limited.

Practice 5   Parallelogram, Rhombus, and Trapezoid

Complete. Figure _ABCD_ is a parallelogram. Measure the sides and angles of the figure.

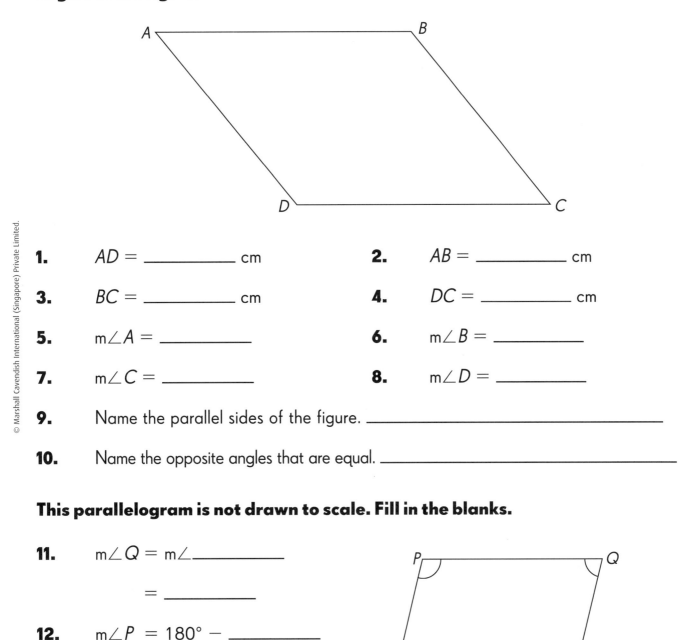

1. $AD =$ _____ cm

2. $AB =$ _____ cm

3. $BC =$ _____ cm

4. $DC =$ _____ cm

5. $m\angle A =$ _____

6. $m\angle B =$ _____

7. $m\angle C =$ _____

8. $m\angle D =$ _____

9.   Name the parallel sides of the figure. _____

10. Name the opposite angles that are equal. _____

This parallelogram is not drawn to scale. Fill in the blanks.

11. $m\angle Q = m\angle$ _____

       $=$ _____

12. $m\angle P = 180° -$ _____

       $=$ _____

13. $m\angle R = m\angle$ _____

       $=$ _____

These parallelograms are not drawn to scale.
Find the unknown angle measures.

14.

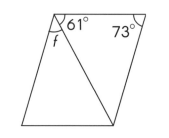

56°

a

15.

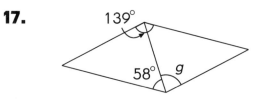

135°

b

16.

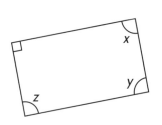

61° 73°

f

17.

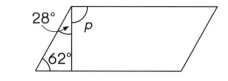

139°

58° g

18.

x

y

z

19.

28°

p

62°

Complete. Write the name of another side or angle of each rhombus.

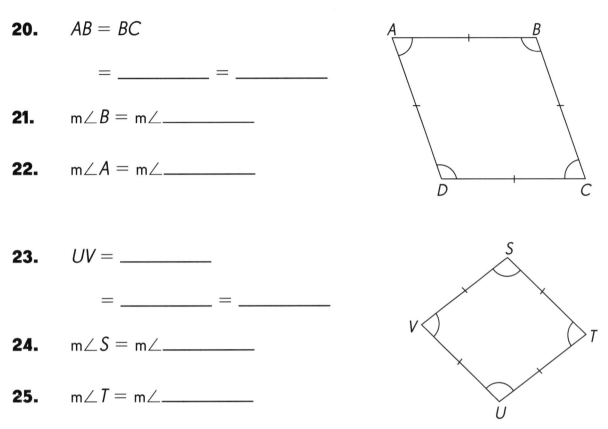

20. $AB = BC$

   = _____ = _____

21. $m\angle B = m\angle$_____

22. $m\angle A = m\angle$_____

23. $UV =$ _____

   = _____ = _____

24. $m\angle S = m\angle$_____

25. $m\angle T = m\angle$_____

This rhombus is not drawn to scale. Fill in the blanks.

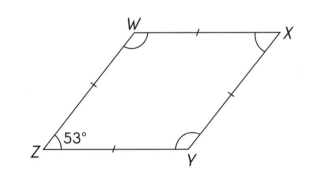

26. $m\angle X = m\angle$ _____ = _____

27. $m\angle W =$_____ − _____ = _____

28. $m\angle Y = m\angle$_____ = _____

These rhombuses are not drawn to scale.
Find the unknown angle measures.

29.

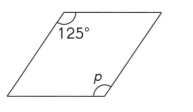

125°

p

30.

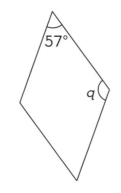

57°

q

31.

129°   r

32.

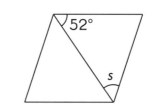

52°

s

33.

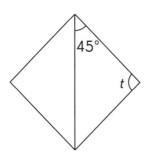

45°

t

34.

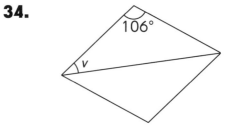

106°

v

Measure the unknown angles. Then fill in the blanks.

***ABCD* is a trapezoid where $\overline{AB} \parallel \overline{DC}$.**

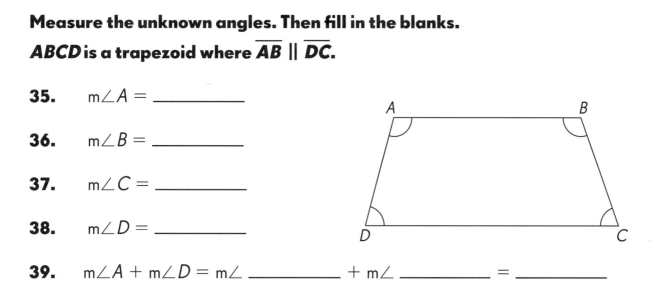

35.   m∠A = _____

36.   m∠B = _____

37.   m∠C = _____

38.   m∠D = _____

39.   m∠A + m∠D = m∠ _____ + m∠ _____ = _____

These trapezoids are not drawn to scale.
Find the unknown angle measures.

40. $\overline{AB} \parallel \overline{DC}$

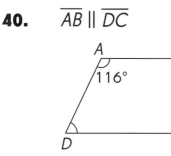

41. $\overline{EH} \parallel \overline{FG}$

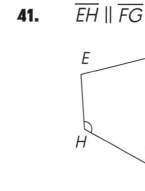

42. $\overline{JK} \parallel \overline{ML}$

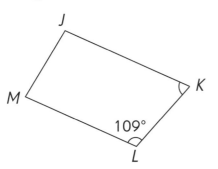

43. $\overline{PS} \parallel \overline{QR}$

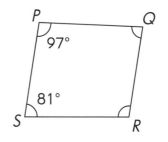

These trapezoids are not drawn to scale.
Find the unknown angle measures.

44. $\overline{TU} \parallel \overline{WV}$

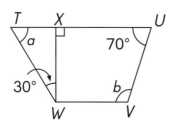

45. $\overline{VW} \parallel \overline{YX}$

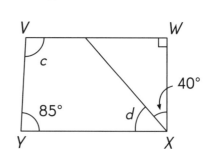

46. $\overline{AB} \parallel \overline{DC}$

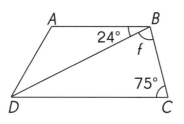

47. $\overline{EH} \parallel \overline{FG}$

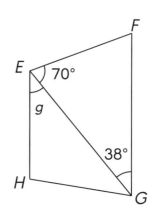

Put On Your Thinking Cap!

Challenging Practice

This figure is a rhombus and $\angle ADO = \angle CDO$. Find the measure of $\angle DOC$.

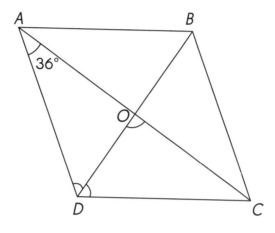

1. *ABCD* is a trapezoid in which $\overline{AD} \parallel \overline{BC}$. Find the measure of $\angle CED$.

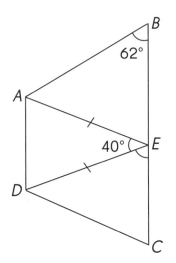

2. *ABCD* is a parallelogram and *CDEF* is a rhombus. Find the measure of $\angle ADE$.

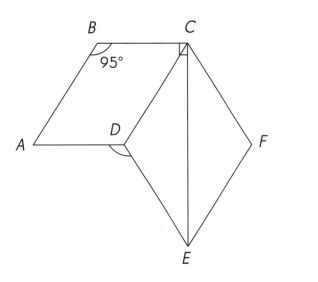

Name: _____   Date: _____

14 Surface Area and Volume

Practice 1   Building Solids Using Unit Cubes

Find the number of unit cubes used to build each solid. Some of the cubes may be hidden.

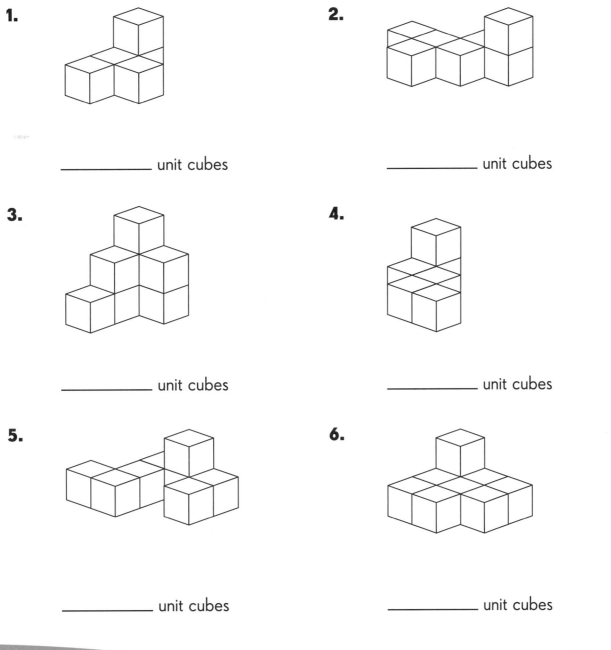

1.

_____ unit cubes

2.

_____ unit cubes

3.

_____ unit cubes

4.

_____ unit cubes

5.

_____ unit cubes

6.

_____ unit cubes

Find the number of unit cubes used to build each solid. Some of the cubes may be hidden.

7.

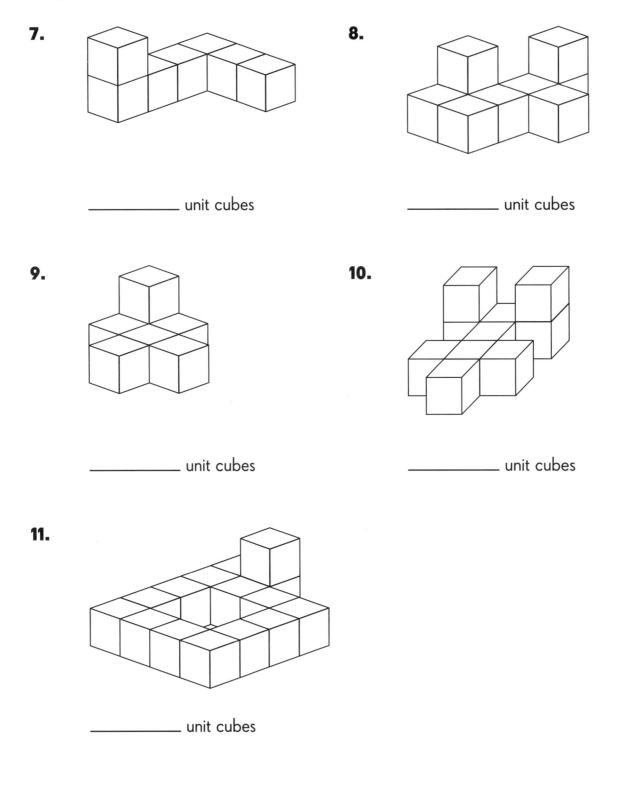

_____ unit cubes

8.

_____ unit cubes

9.

_____ unit cubes

10.

_____ unit cubes

11.

_____ unit cubes

Practice 2   Drawing Cubes and Rectangular Prisms

Draw on dot paper.

1.   Draw a unit cube.

2.   Draw two different views of a rectangular prism made up of 2 unit cubes.

3.   Draw two different solids made up of 3 unit cubes each.

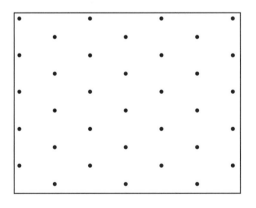
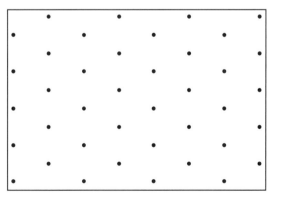

Draw each cube or rectangular prism on the dot paper.

Example

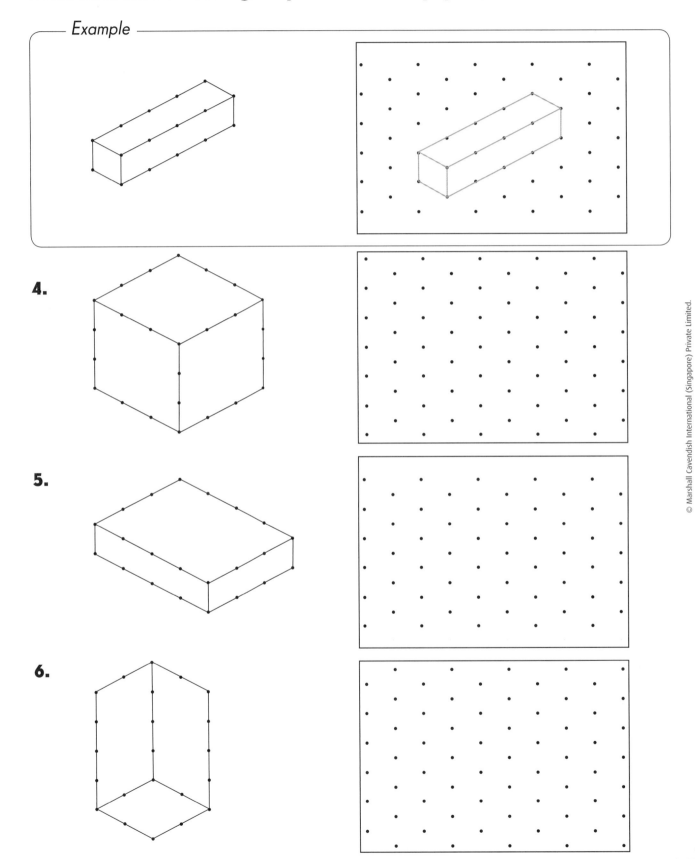

4.

5.

6.

Draw each cube or rectangular prism on the dot paper.

7.

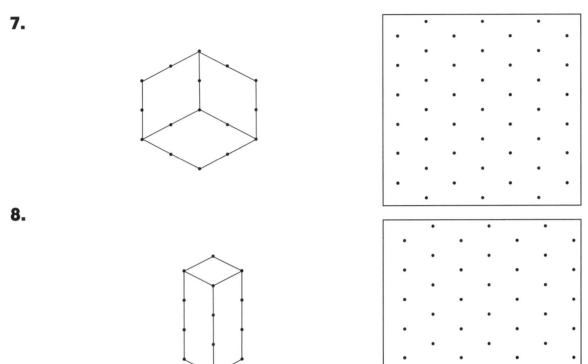

8.

Draw a cube with edges 4 times as long as the edges of this unit cube.

9.

Complete the drawing of each cube or rectangular prism.

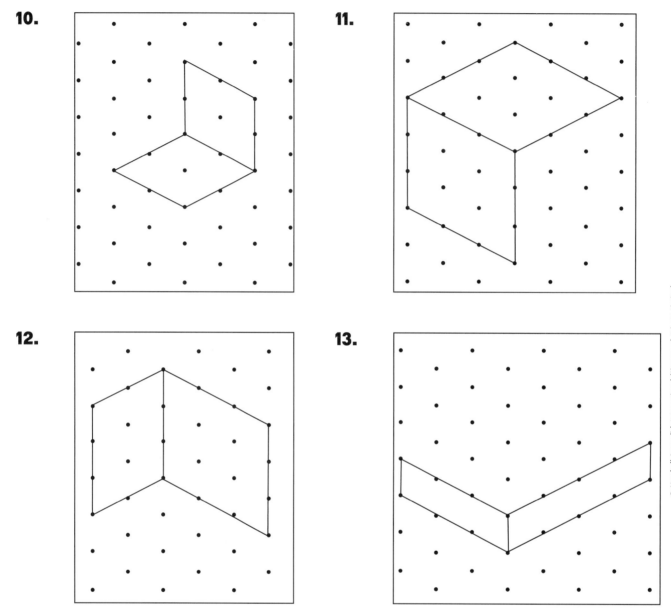

10.

11.

12.

13.

Practice 3 Prisms and Pyramids

Identify the type of prism and the shapes of the faces.

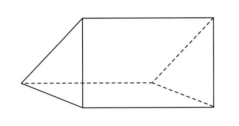

1. This is a _____ prism.

2. Two of its faces are _____.

3. Three of its faces are _____.

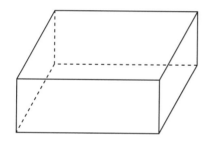

4. This is a _____ prism.

5. All its faces are _____.

Complete the table.

Type of Prism	Number of Faces	Number of Edges	Number of Vertices
6. 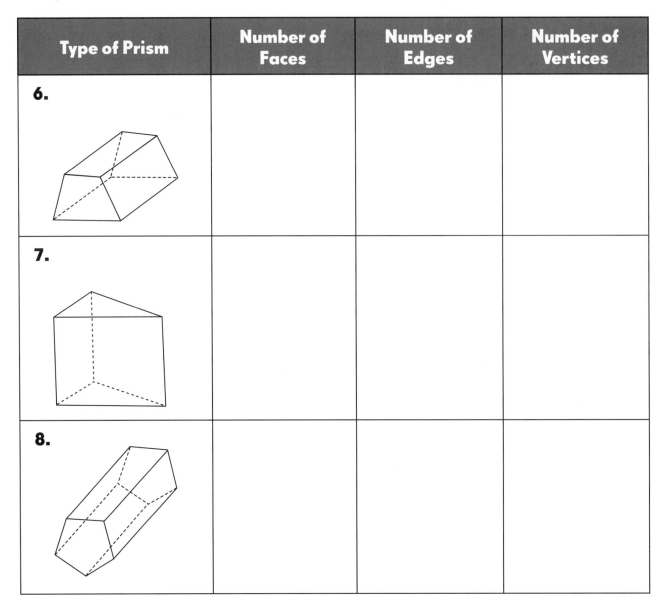			
7.			
8.			

Identify the type of pyramid and the shape of the faces.

9. This is a _____ pyramid.

10. All its faces are _____.

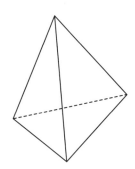

Identify the type of pyramid and the shapes of the faces.

11.   This is a _____ pyramid.

12.   One of its faces is a _____.

13.   Four of its faces are _____.

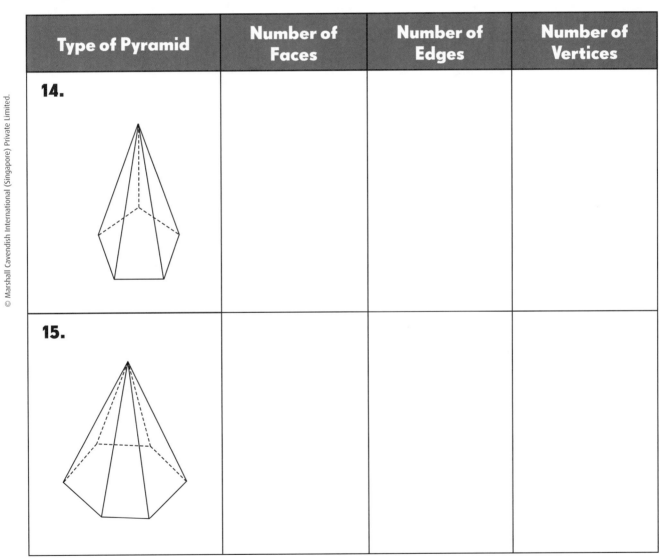

Complete the table.

Type of Pyramid	Number of Faces	Number of Edges	Number of Vertices
14. 			
15.			

Name the solid formed by each net.

16.

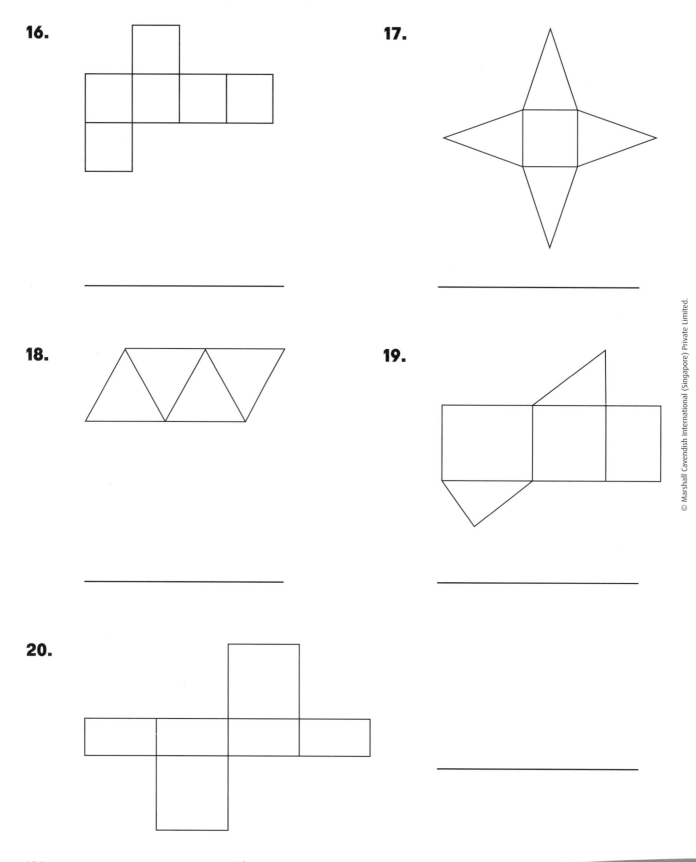

_____

17.

_____

18.

_____

19.

_____

20.

_____

Practice 4   Nets and Surface Area

Find the surface area of each cube.

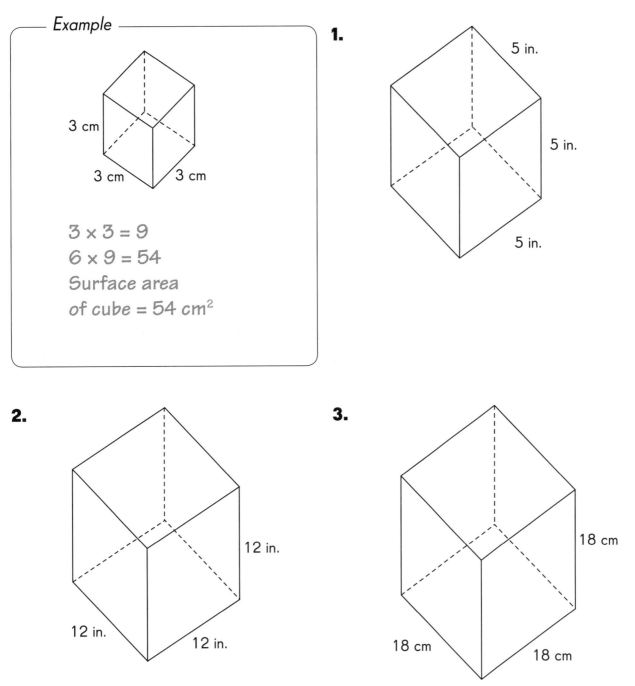

Example

3 cm

3 cm   3 cm

$3 \times 3 = 9$
$6 \times 9 = 54$
Surface area
of cube = 54 cm²

1.

5 in.

5 in.

5 in.

2.

12 in.

12 in.   12 in.

3.

18 cm

18 cm   18 cm

Find the surface area of each rectangular prism.

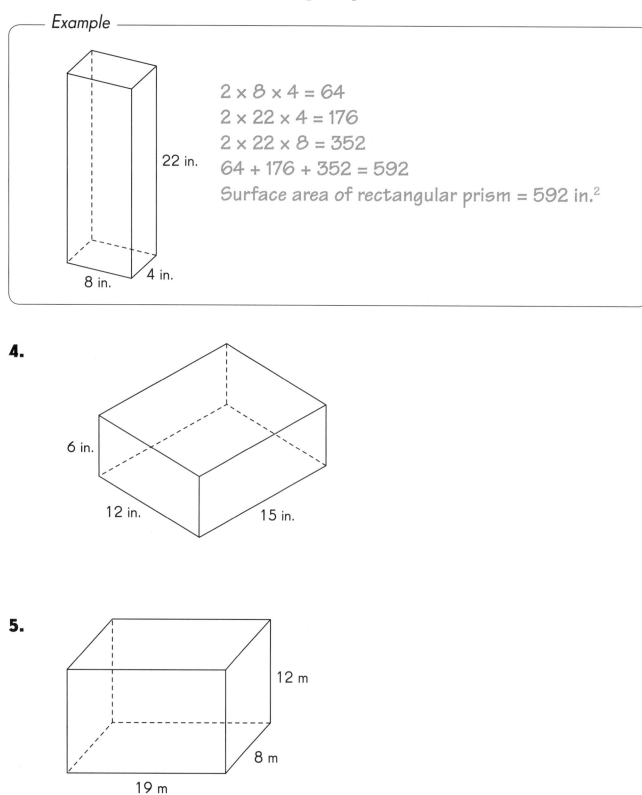

Example

$2 \times 8 \times 4 = 64$
$2 \times 22 \times 4 = 176$
$2 \times 22 \times 8 = 352$
$64 + 176 + 352 = 592$
Surface area of rectangular prism = 592 in.^{2}

22 in.

8 in.   4 in.

4.

6 in.

12 in.   15 in.

5.

12 m

8 m

19 m

Find the surface area of each triangular prism.

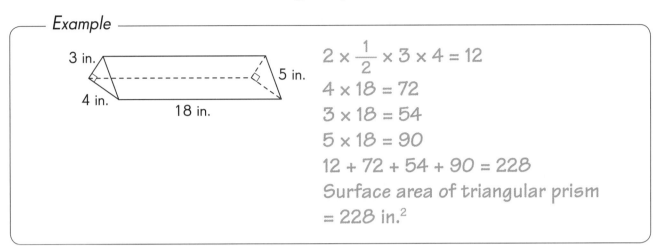

Example

3 in.
5 in.
4 in.
18 in.

$2 \times \dfrac{1}{2} \times 3 \times 4 = 12$

$4 \times 18 = 72$

$3 \times 18 = 54$

$5 \times 18 = 90$

$12 + 72 + 54 + 90 = 228$

Surface area of triangular prism

$= 228 \text{ in.}^2$

6.

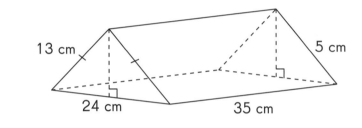

13 cm   5 cm
24 cm   35 cm

Solve. Show your work.

7.   Jeffrey cuts out the net of a box he wants to make.
       Find the surface area of the box.

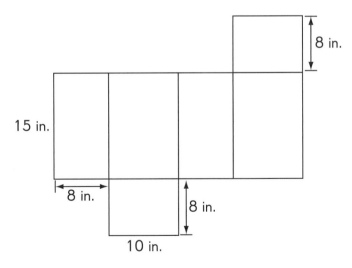

8 in.

15 in.

8 in.

8 in.

10 in.

Solve. Show your work.

8. This glass fish tank does not have a cover. Find the total area of the glass panels used to make the tank.

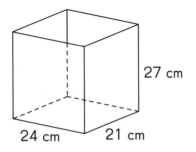

27 cm

24 cm   21 cm

9. The tank shown is made of steel. It does not have a cover. Find the area of steel sheet used to make the tank.

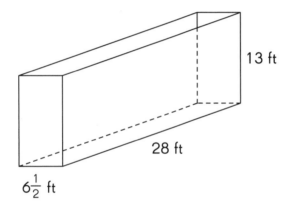

13 ft

28 ft

$6\frac{1}{2}$ ft

10. A rectangular piece of poster board measures 60 centimeters by 80 centimeters. Linn draws the net of a box on the poster board and cuts it out. If the box measures 10 centimeters by 16 centimeters by 27 centimeters, what is the area of the poster board left?

Practice 5   Understanding and Measuring Volume

**These solids are formed by stacking unit cubes in the corner of a box.
Find the volume of each solid.**

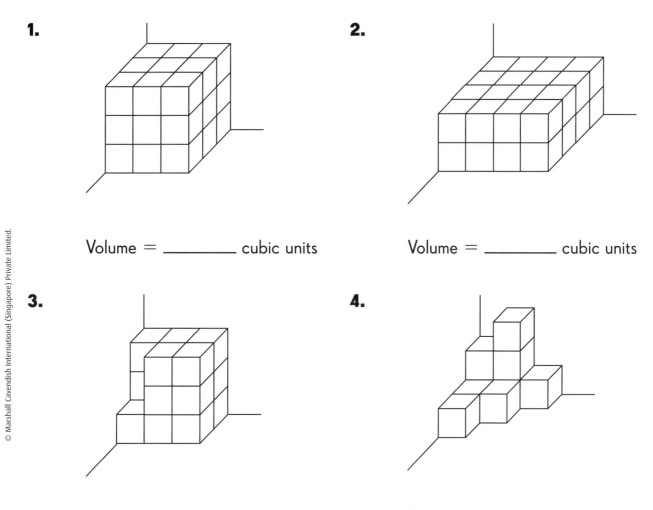

1.

Volume = _____ cubic units

2.

Volume = _____ cubic units

3.

Volume = _____ cubic units

4.

Volume = _____ cubic units

These solids are formed by stacking 1-centimeter cubes in the corner of a box. Find the volume of each solid.

5.

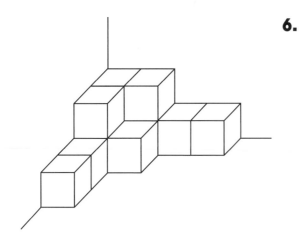

Volume = _____ cm³

6.

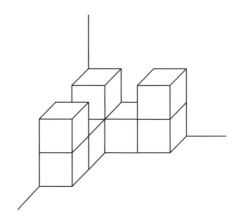

Volume = _____ cm³

7.

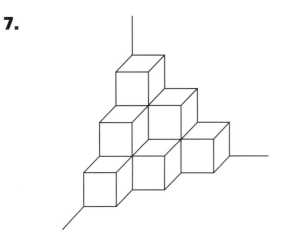

Volume = _____ cm³

8.

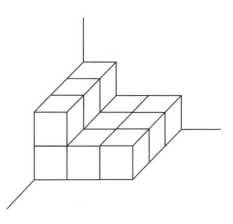

Volume = _____ cm³

9.

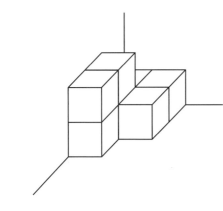

Volume = _____ cm³

10.

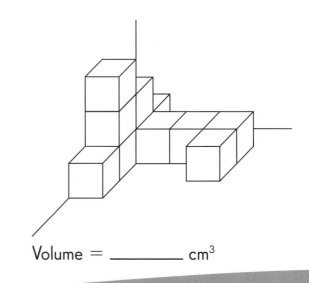

Volume = _____ cm³

These solids are built using 1-centimeter cubes. Find the volume of each solid. Then compare their volumes and fill in the blanks.

11.

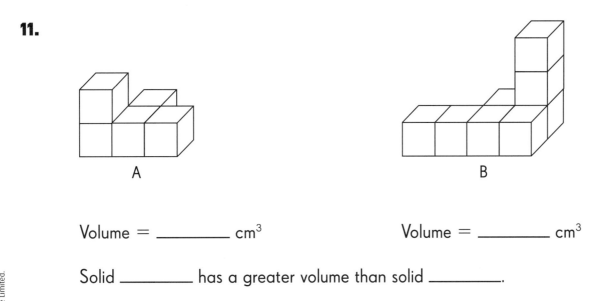

A

B

Volume = _____ cm³

Volume = _____ cm³

Solid _____ has a greater volume than solid _____.

These solids are built using 1-meter cubes. Find the volume of each solid. Then compare their volumes and fill in the blanks.

12.

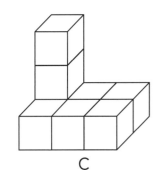

C

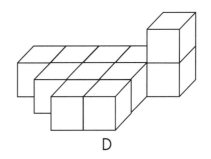

D

Volume = _____ m³

Volume = _____ m³

Solid _____ has a lesser volume than solid _____.

These solids are built using 1-inch cubes. Find the volume of each solid. Then compare their volumes and fill in the blanks.

13.

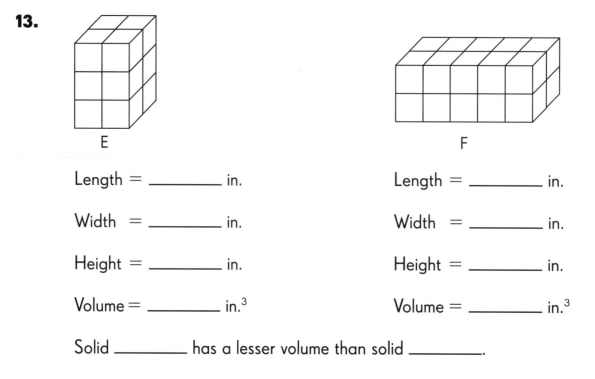

E

Length = _____ in.

Width = _____ in.

Height = _____ in.

Volume = _____ in.^{3}

F

Length = _____ in.

Width = _____ in.

Height = _____ in.

Volume = _____ in.^{3}

Solid _____ has a lesser volume than solid _____.

These solids are built using 1-foot cubes. Find the volume of each solid. Then compare their volumes and fill in the blanks.

14.

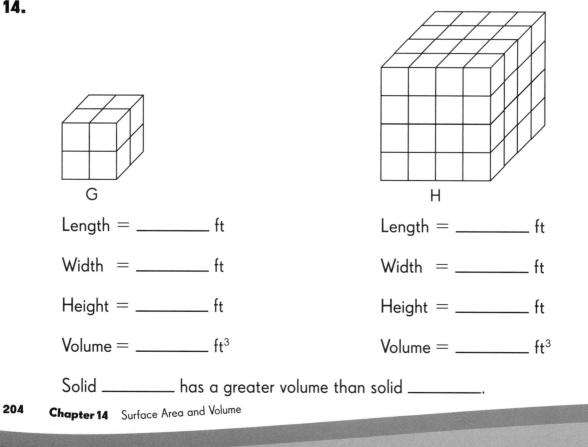

G

Length = _____ ft

Width = _____ ft

Height = _____ ft

Volume = _____ ft^3

H

Length = _____ ft

Width = _____ ft

Height = _____ ft

Volume = _____ ft^3

Solid _____ has a greater volume than solid _____.

Practice 6   Volume of a Rectangular Prism and Liquid

Write the length, width, and height of each rectangular prism or cube.

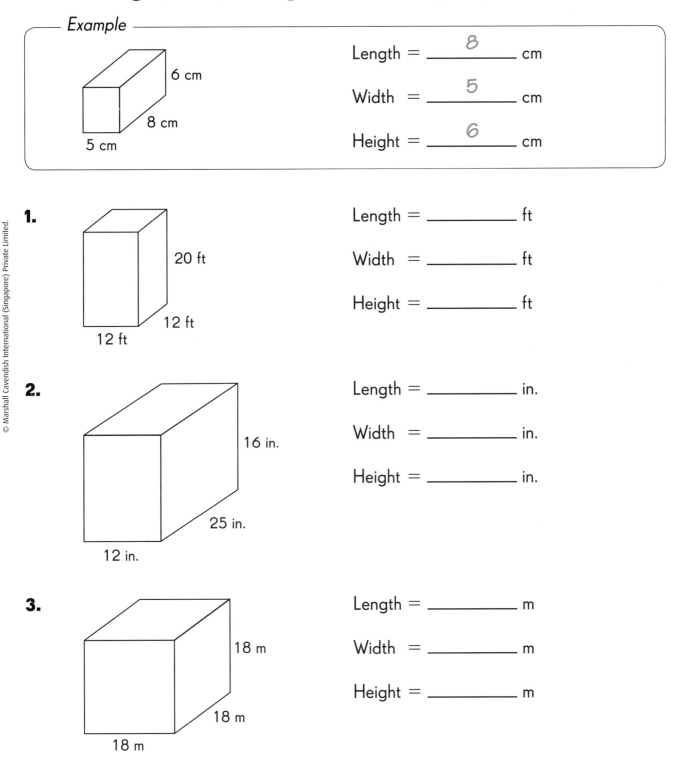

Example

6 cm
8 cm
5 cm

Length = _____8_____ cm

Width = _____5_____ cm

Height = _____6_____ cm

1.

20 ft
12 ft
12 ft

Length = _____ ft

Width = _____ ft

Height = _____ ft

2.

16 in.
25 in.
12 in.

Length = _____ in.

Width = _____ in.

Height = _____ in.

3.

18 m
18 m
18 m

Length = _____ m

Width = _____ m

Height = _____ m

Find the volume of each rectangular prism.

4.

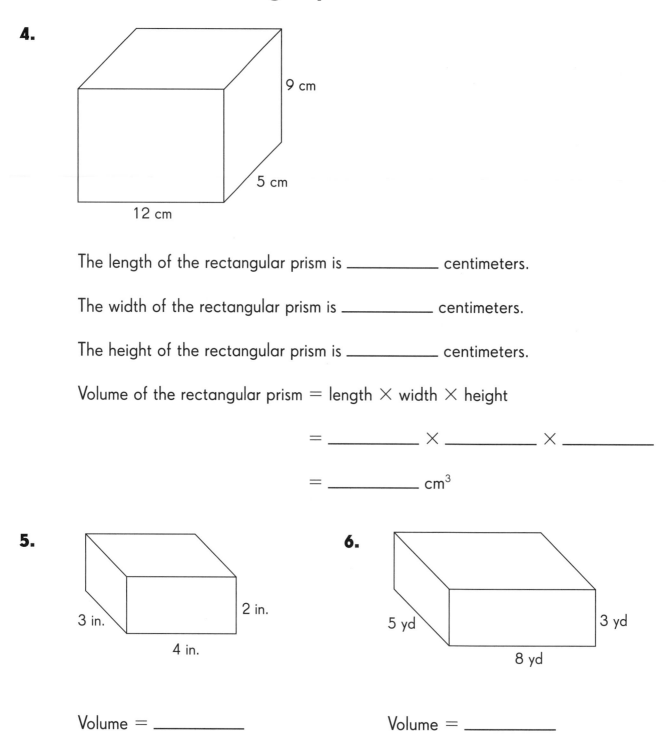

The length of the rectangular prism is _____ centimeters.

The width of the rectangular prism is _____ centimeters.

The height of the rectangular prism is _____ centimeters.

Volume of the rectangular prism = length × width × height

                     = _____ × _____ × _____

                     = _____ cm^3

5.

Volume = _____

6.

Volume = _____

Find the volume of each rectangular prism or cube.

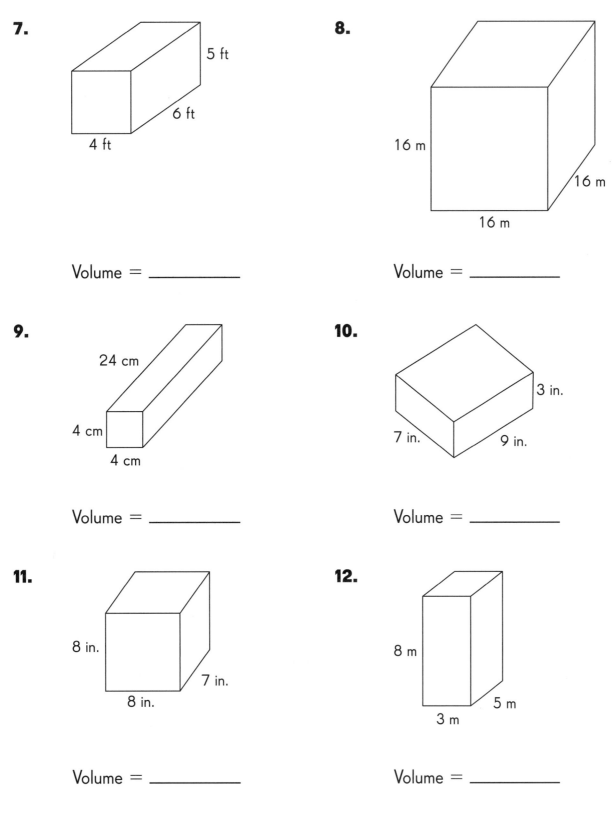

7.

5 ft

6 ft

4 ft

Volume = _____

8.

16 m

16 m

16 m

Volume = _____

9.

24 cm

4 cm

4 cm

Volume = _____

10.

3 in.

7 in.

9 in.

Volume = _____

11.

8 in.

7 in.

8 in.

Volume = _____

12.

8 m

5 m

3 m

Volume = _____

Find the volume of each rectangular prism.

	Length	Width	Height	Volume
13.	5 cm	12 cm	9 cm	
14.	10 in.	25 in.	14 in.	
15.	7 m	12 m	8 m	
16.	24 ft	10 ft	15 ft	

Solve. Show your work.

17. Find the volume of a cube with edges measuring 9 centimeters.

18. A rectangular prism has a length of 8 feet and a height of 5 feet. Its length is twice its width. Find the volume of the rectangular prism.

19. The base of a rectangular prism is a square whose sides each measure 9 inches. The height of the rectangular prism is 11 inches. Find its volume.

Find the volume of each rectangular prism.

Example

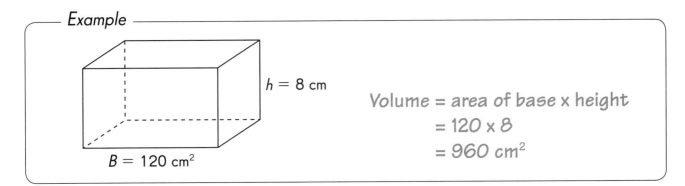

$h = 8$ cm

$B = 120$ cm^2

Volume = area of base x height
= 120 x 8
= 960 cm^2

20.

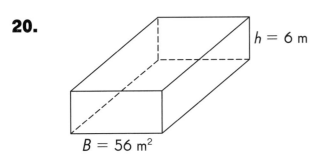

$h = 6$ m

$B = 56$ m^2

21.

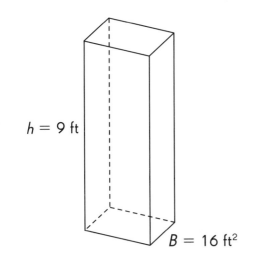

$h = 9$ ft

$B = 16$ ft^2

22.

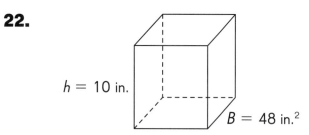

$h = 10$ in.

$B = 48$ in.^{2}

23.

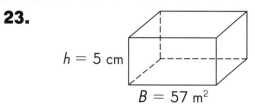

$h = 5$ cm

$B = 57$ m^2

Solve. Show your work.

24.   A rectangular box has a height of 15 meters. The area of its base is 210 square meters. Find the volume of the box.

25.   Gerald's rectangular container has a height of 6 feet and a base area of 72 square feet. How much water would it take to fill the container to the brim?

Practice 7   Volume of a Rectangular Prism and Liquid

Write each measure in milliliters.

1.   690 cm³ = _____

2.   207 cm³ = _____

3.   2,000 cm³ = _____

4.   4,600 cm³ = _____

Write each measure in cubic centimeters.

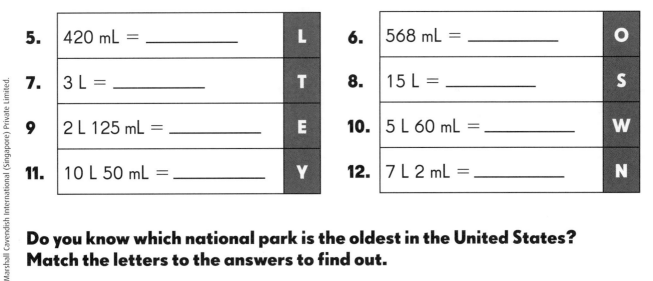

5.   420 mL = _____   **L**

6.   568 mL = _____   **O**

7.   3 L = _____   **T**

8.   15 L = _____   **S**

9   2 L 125 mL = _____   **E**

10.   5 L 60 mL = _____   **W**

11.   10 L 50 mL = _____   **Y**

12.   7 L 2 mL = _____   **N**

Do you know which national park is the oldest in the United States? Match the letters to the answers to find out.

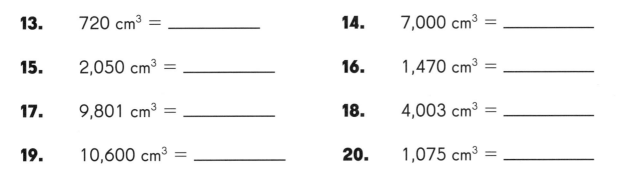

_____ _____ _____ _____ _____ _____ _____ _____ _____ _____ _____

10,050 2,125   420   420   568   5,060 15,000 3,000   568   7,002 2,125

National Park

Write each measure in liters and milliliters.

13.   720 cm³ = _____

14.   7,000 cm³ = _____

15.   2,050 cm³ = _____

16.   1,470 cm³ = _____

17.   9,801 cm³ = _____

18.   4,003 cm³ = _____

19.   10,600 cm³ = _____

20.   1,075 cm³ = _____

Find the volume of water in each rectangular tank in milliliters.
(Hint: 1 cm³ = 1 mL)

21.

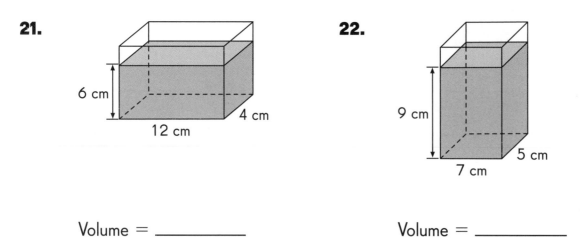

6 cm
12 cm
4 cm

Volume = _____

22.

9 cm
7 cm
5 cm

Volume = _____

Find the volume of water in each rectangular tank in liters and milliliters.
(Hint: 1,000 cm³ = 1 L)

23.

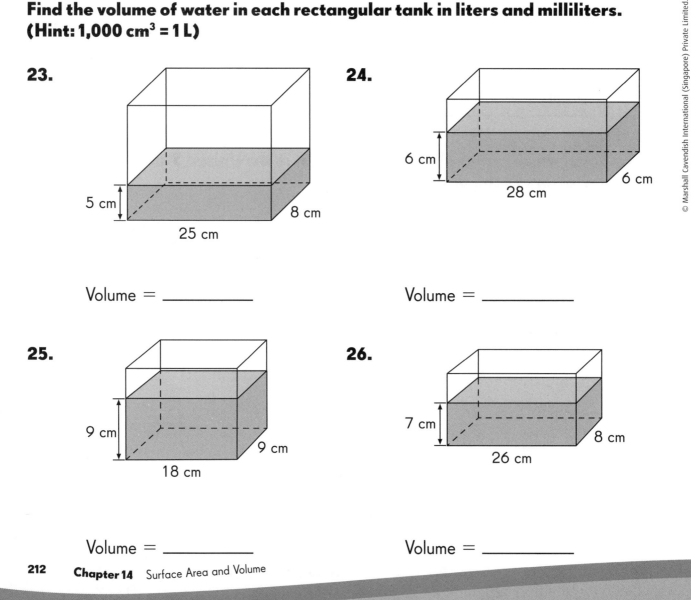

5 cm
25 cm
8 cm

Volume = _____

24.

6 cm
28 cm
6 cm

Volume = _____

25.

9 cm
18 cm
9 cm

Volume = _____

26.

7 cm
26 cm
8 cm

Volume = _____

Solve. Show your work.

27. How much water is in this tank when it is $\frac{1}{3}$ full?

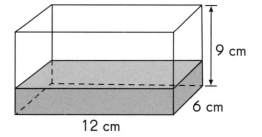

28. This rectangular tank is filled with water to a height of 4 centimeters. How much more water is needed to fill the tank completely?

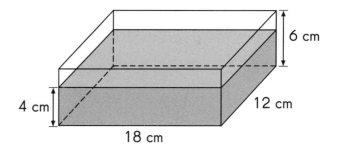

Solve. Show your work.

29. A cubical tank with an edge length of 20 centimeters is filled with 3.75 liters of water. How much more water is needed to fill the tank completely? Give your answer in liters.

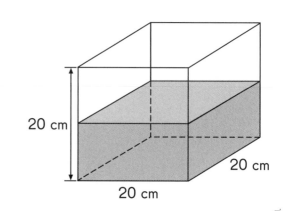

30. The rectangular tank shown is $\frac{1}{4}$-filled with water. Then another 1 liter 400 milliliters of water is added. Find the volume of water in the tank in the end. Give your answer in liters and milliliters.

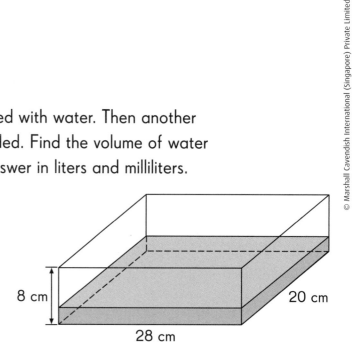

Solve. Show your work.

31. This container is half-filled with oil. What is the volume of oil in the container? Give your answer in liters and milliliters.

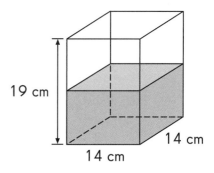

32. A cubical tank whose edges each measure 12 centimeters is half-filled with water. The water is poured into an empty rectangular tank measuring 10 centimeters by 8 centimeters by 7 centimeters until it is full. How much water is left in the cubical tank? Give your answer in milliliters.

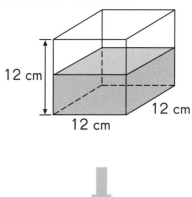

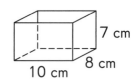

Solve. Show your work.

33. The rectangular swimming pool shown contains 600 cubic meters of water. How much more water has to be added so that the water level is 1 meter from the top?

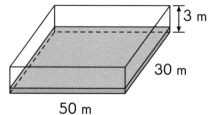

34. The rectangular tank shown is filled completely with water. How much water must be taken out so the height of the water level in the tank is 10 centimeters? Give your answer in milliliters.

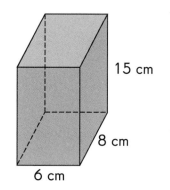

Solve. Show your work.

35. The large rectangular tank shown is $\frac{4}{5}$-filled with water.
The water is then poured into the smaller rectangular container
until it is full. How much water is left in the tank? Give your answer
in liters and milliliters.

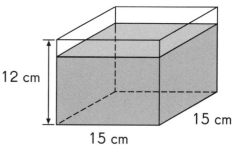

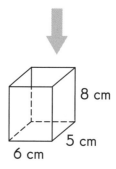

36. Water flows into this tank at 8 liters per minute.
How long will it take to fill the tank?

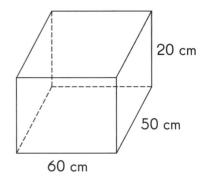

20 cm

50 cm

60 cm

Practice 8 Volume of Composite Solids

Find the volume of each solid figure.

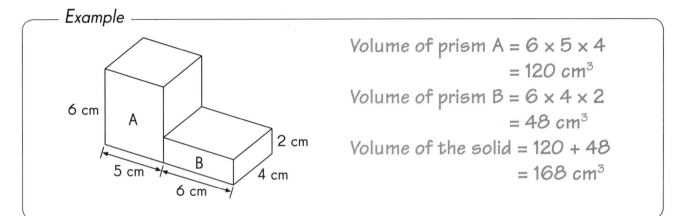

— *Example* —

6 cm

A

5 cm

B

6 cm

4 cm

2 cm

Volume of prism A = 6 × 5 × 4
= 120 cm³
Volume of prism B = 6 × 4 × 2
= 48 cm³
Volume of the solid = 120 + 48
= 168 cm³

1.

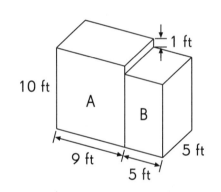

1 ft

10 ft

A

B

9 ft

5 ft

5 ft

Volume of prism A =

Volume of prism B =

Volume of the solid = _____ + _____

= _____ ft³

2.

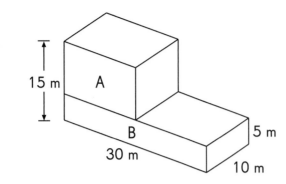

Volume of prism A =

Volume of prism B =

Volume of the solid = _____ + _____

= _____ m³

Solve. Show your work.

3.

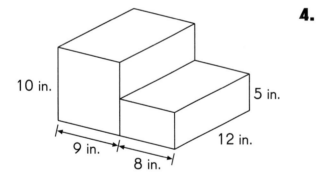

Volume = _____

4.

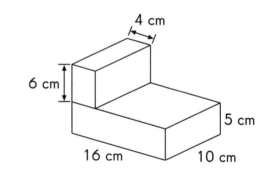

Volume = _____

5.   A rectangular block of wood is cut into two pieces, as shown below. What is the total volume of the block of wood?

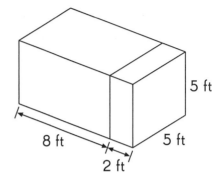

Solve. Show your work.

6.   A shelf is made up of two rectangular pieces of metal. What is the total volume of metal in the shelf?

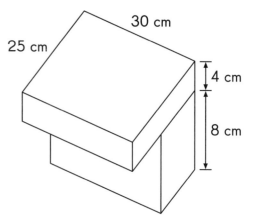

Math Journal

This rectangular container is $\frac{2}{5}$-filled with water. How much more water is needed to increase the height of the water level to 3 centimeters?

Show two methods of solving this problem. Which method do you prefer? Why?

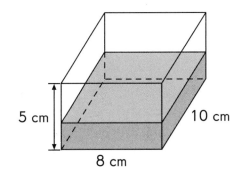

5 cm

10 cm

8 cm

Put On Your Thinking Cap!

Challenging Practice

Find the number of cubes in each prism.

1.

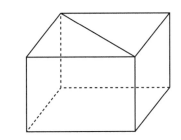

_____ cubes

2.

_____ cubes

Each solid is cut vertically along the line shown. Draw an additional line to complete the two shapes. Then, identify the solid shapes that result.

3.

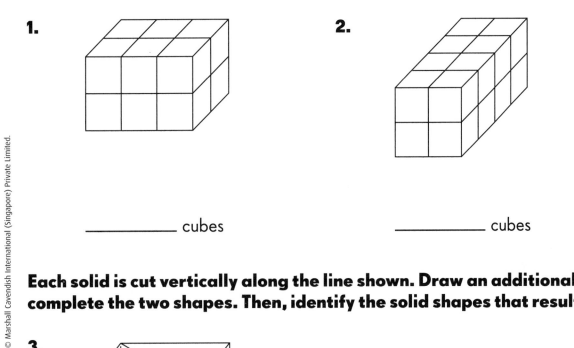

_____

4.

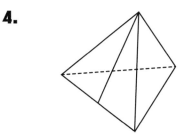

_____

5. A rectangular tank is half-filled with water. Another 650 cubic centimeters of water are needed to make it $\frac{3}{5}$ full. How much water will be in the tank when it is $\frac{3}{5}$ full?

6. A cube has a surface area of 216 square centimeters.
A second cube has edges that are 3 times as long. How much greater is the surface area of the second cube than the first cube?

Put On Your Thinking Cap!

Problem Solving

You may trace, cut out, and fold the nets.

Which of these are nets of a cube? Check the boxes.

1.

2.

3.

4.

5.

6.

7.

8.

9. A prism has a square base whose edges each measure
5 centimeters. The ratio of its height to its width is 4 : 1.
Find the volume of the rectangular prism in cubic centimeters.

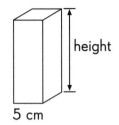

height

5 cm

Name: _____   **Date:** _____

for Chapter 13 and 14

Concepts and Skills

Find the unknown angle measures. Then classify triangle *ABC* as an acute, obtuse, or right triangle. *(Lessons 13.1 to 13.3)*

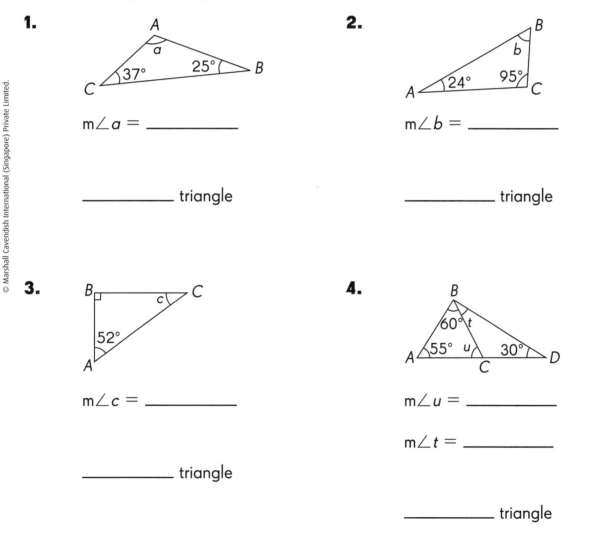

1.

m∠a = _____

_____ triangle

2.

m∠b = _____

_____ triangle

3.

m∠c = _____

_____ triangle

4.

m∠u = _____

m∠t = _____

_____ triangle

Find the unknown angle measures. The figures are not drawn to scale.

(Lesson 13.3)

5.

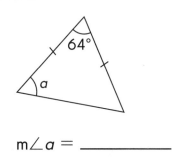

m∠a = _____

6.

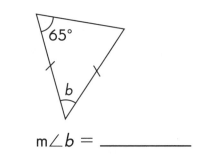

m∠b = _____

7. AB = BC = AD

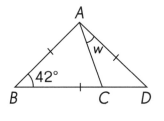

m∠w = _____

8.

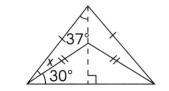

m∠x = _____

9.

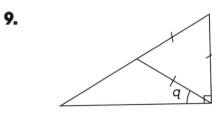

m∠q = _____

10. ZY = YX = XZ

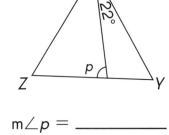

m∠p = _____

Name: _____   **Date:** _____

Measure the sides of the triangles in inches. Then fill in the blanks.

(Lessons 13.1 and 13.4)

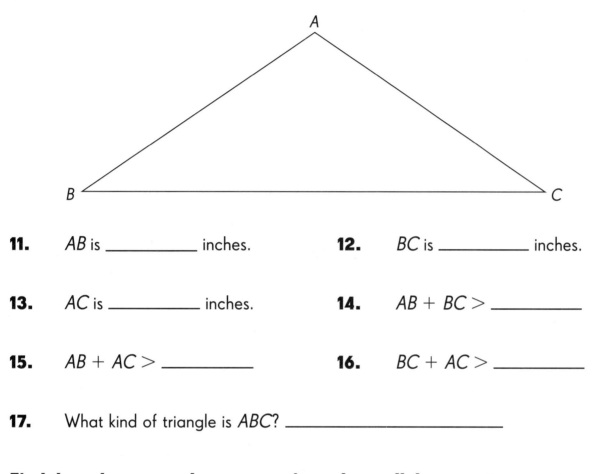

11.   *AB* is _____ inches.   **12.**   *BC* is _____ inches.

13.   *AC* is _____ inches.   **14.**   *AB* + *BC* > _____

15.   *AB* + *AC* > _____   **16.**   *BC* + *AC* > _____

17.   What kind of triangle is *ABC*? _____

Find the unknown angle measures in each parallelogram. (Lesson 13.5)

18.

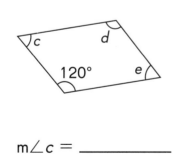

19.

m∠*c* = _____   m∠*f* = _____

m∠*d* = _____

m∠*e* = _____

Find the unknown angle measures in each rhombus. *(Lesson 13.5)*

20.

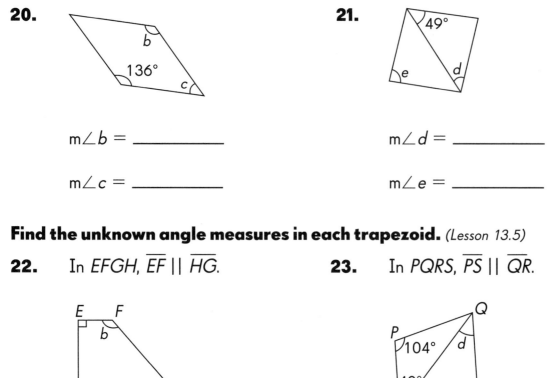

m∠b = _____

m∠c = _____

21.

49°

e   d

m∠d = _____

m∠e = _____

Find the unknown angle measures in each trapezoid. *(Lesson 13.5)*

22.   In *EFGH*, $\overline{EF} \parallel \overline{HG}$.

E   F
    b

c   46°
H   G

m∠b = _____

m∠c = _____

23.   In *PQRS*, $\overline{PS} \parallel \overline{QR}$.

P   Q
  104°   d

  40°

S
         R

m∠d = _____

Find how many unit cubes are used to build each solid. *(Lesson 14.1)*

24.

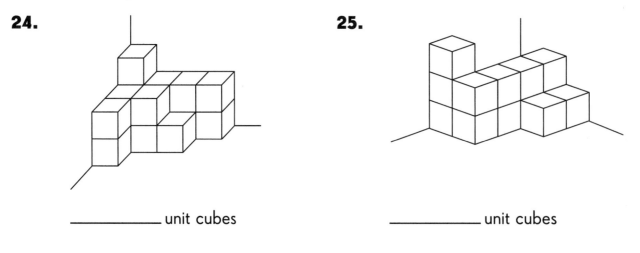

_____ unit cubes

25.

_____ unit cubes

Draw a cube with edges 2 times as long as the edges of this unit cube. *(Lesson 14.2)*

26.

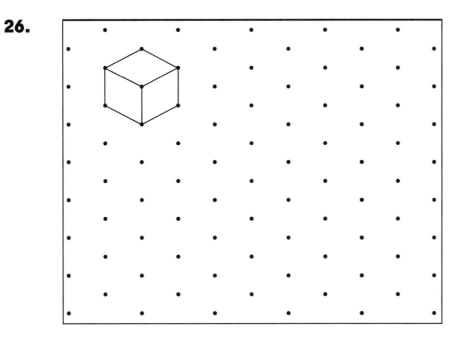

Complete the drawing of this rectangular prism. *(Lesson 14.2)*

27.

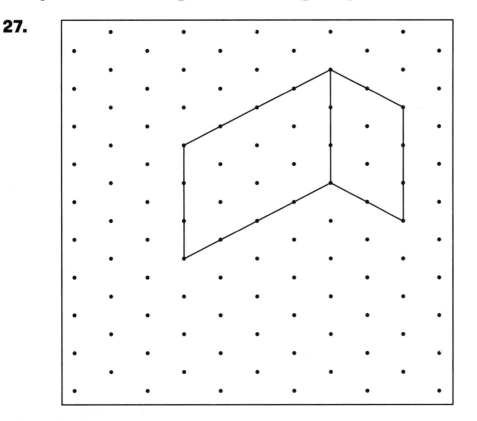

Name each solid. Then write the number of faces and vertices, and the shapes of the faces. (Lesson 14.3)

Solid	Number of Faces	Number of Vertices	Shapes of Faces
28. 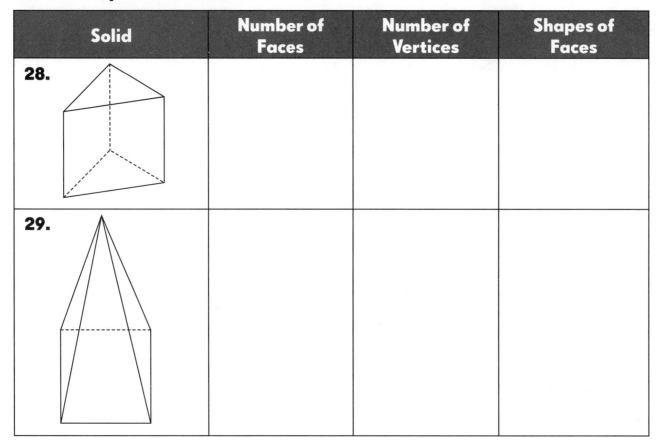			
29.			

Name the solid formed from each net. (Lesson 14.3)

30. **31.**

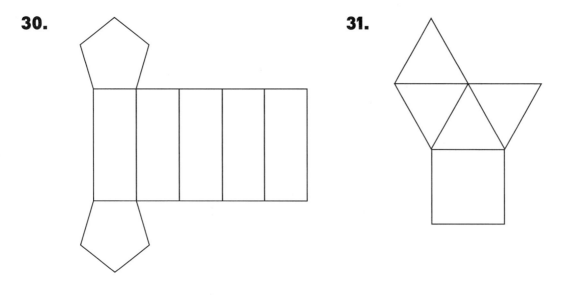

_____   _____

Find the surface area of each prism. *(Lesson 14.4)*

32.

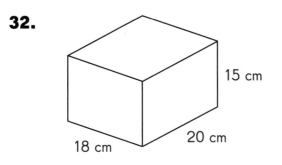

15 cm

20 cm

18 cm

33.

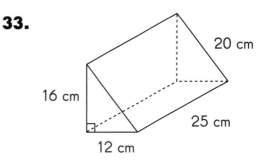

20 cm

16 cm

25 cm

12 cm

These solids are built using 1-inch cubes. Find and compare their volumes.

(Lesson 14.5)

34.

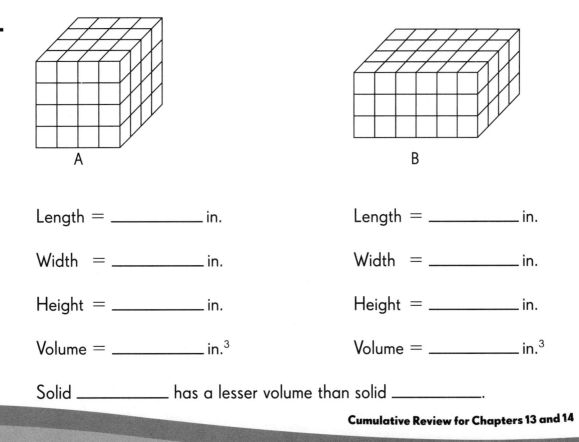

A

B

Length = _____ in.   Length = _____ in.

Width = _____ in.   Width = _____ in.

Height = _____ in.   Height = _____ in.

Volume = _____ in.³   Volume = _____ in.³

Solid _____ has a lesser volume than solid _____.

Find the volume of each rectangular prism. *(Lesson 14.6)*

35.

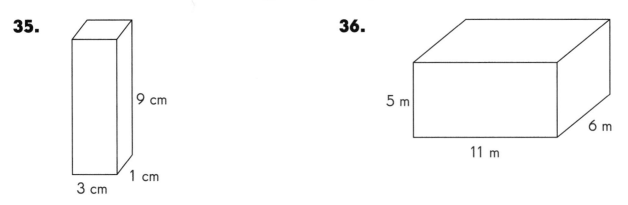

9 cm

1 cm

3 cm

36.

5 m

11 m

6 m

Find the volume of water in each container in liters and milliliters.

(Lesson 14.6)

37.

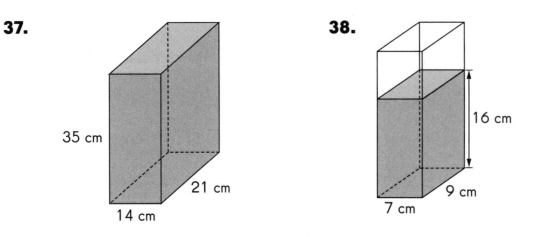

35 cm

21 cm

14 cm

38.

16 cm

7 cm

9 cm

Find the volume of each rectangular prism. (*Lesson 14.6*)

39.

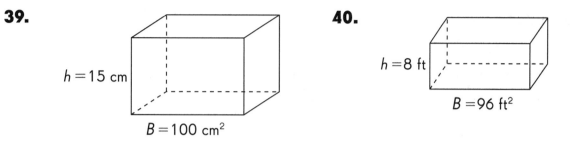

$h = 15$ cm

$B = 100$ cm^2

40.

$h = 8$ ft

$B = 96$ ft^2

Find the volume of each solid. (*Lesson 14.7*)

41.

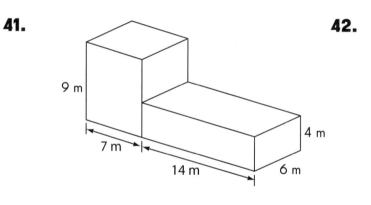

9 m

7 m

14 m

4 m

6 m

42.

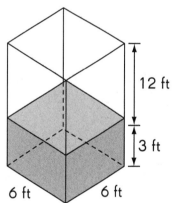

12 ft

3 ft

6 ft   6 ft

Problem Solving

Solve. Show your work.

43.   In the triangle ABC, $AB = 4$ centimeters, $BC = 7$ centimeters, and AC is longer than 8 centimeters. If the length of $\overline{AC}$ is in whole centimeters, what are the possible lengths of $\overline{AC}$?

44. $ABCD$ is a trapezoid and $ABED$ is a parallelogram. $\overline{AB} \parallel \overline{DC}$, $\overline{AD} \parallel \overline{BE}$, and $BE = BC$. Find the measure of $\angle BCE$.

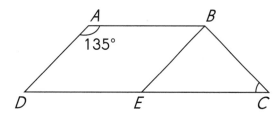

Solve. Show your work.

45. The length of a rectangular block is 20 inches. Its width is half its length. Its height is half its width. What is the surface area of the block?

46. A rectangular piece of poster board measures 70 centimeters by 50 centimeters. The net of a cube with 12-centimeter edges is cut from it. What is the area of the poster board left?

Solve. Show your work.

47. A rectangular prism is 15 inches long and 12 inches high. Its width is $\frac{3}{5}$ its length. Find its volume.

48. Three cubes with edges measuring 5 inches are stacked on top of one another. What is the total volume of the three cubes?

Solve. Show your work.

49. The rectangular container shown contains 2 liters of water.
How much more water must be added to fill the container completely?
Give your answer in liters.

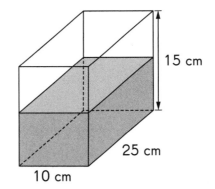

15 cm

25 cm

10 cm

50. A container is 28 centimeters long, 14 centimeters wide, and
10 centimeters high. It is half-filled with juice. Kathy pours 500 milliliters
of water into the container to make a juice drink. Find the volume of
juice drink in the container now. Give your answer in liters and milliliters.

Solve. Show your work.

51. The fish tank shown is filled with 4 liters of water per minute from a faucet. How long does it take to fill the tank completely?

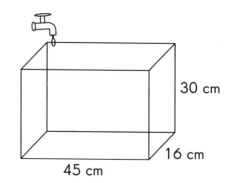

30 cm

16 cm

45 cm

Name: _____   **Date:** _____

End-of-Year Review

Test Prep

Multiple Choice

Shade the circle next to the correct answer.

1. In 130.426, the digit 2 is in the _____ place. *(Lesson 8.1)*

   Ⓐ tens   Ⓑ tenths

   Ⓒ hundredths   Ⓓ thousandths

2. Use front-end estimation with adjustment to estimate
   $6,189 - 3,674$. *(Lesson 1.4)*

   Ⓐ 1,000   Ⓑ 2,000

   Ⓒ 3,000   Ⓓ 4,000

3. Simplify $48 \div 8 + 13 \times 3$. *(Lesson 2.7)*

   Ⓐ 45   Ⓑ 54

   Ⓒ 57   Ⓓ 75

4. Express $10\frac{1}{4} - 4\frac{1}{2}$ as a decimal. *(Lesson 3.3)*

   Ⓐ 6.25   Ⓑ 5.75

   Ⓒ 5.43   Ⓓ 5.34

5. Express 9.062 as a mixed number in simplest form. *(Lesson 8.3)*

   Ⓐ $9\frac{62}{100}$ Ⓑ $9\frac{31}{50}$

   Ⓒ $9\frac{62}{1000}$ Ⓓ $9\frac{31}{500}$

6. What is the product of 96 and 13? *(Lesson 2.4)*

   Ⓐ 900   Ⓑ 960

   Ⓒ 1,170   Ⓓ 1,248

7. Divide 84 by 400. *(Lesson 9.4)*

    Ⓐ 0.21   Ⓑ 0.84

    Ⓒ 2.1   Ⓓ 8.4

8. Simplify $16p + 5 - 3p - 2$. *(Lesson 5.3)*

    Ⓐ $19p + 7$ Ⓑ $19p - 3$

    Ⓒ $13p + 3$ Ⓓ $13p - 3$

9. For what value of y will the inequality $4y - 8 > 10$ be true? *(Lesson 5.4)*

    Ⓐ 2   Ⓑ 3

    Ⓒ 4   Ⓓ 5

10. What percent of the figure is shaded? *(Lesson 10.1)*

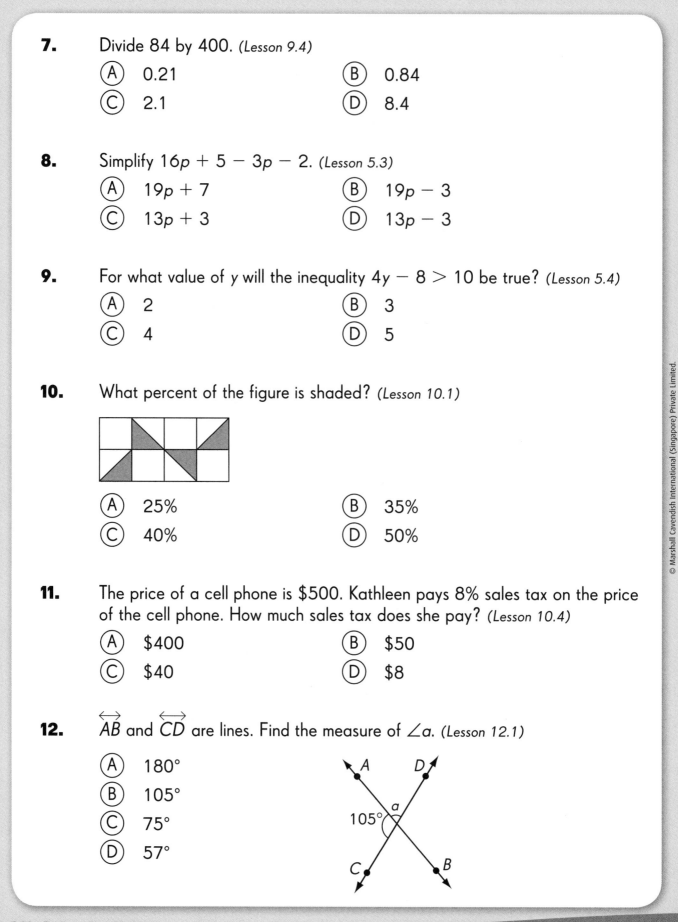

    Ⓐ 25%   Ⓑ 35%

    Ⓒ 40%   Ⓓ 50%

11. The price of a cell phone is $500. Kathleen pays 8% sales tax on the price of the cell phone. How much sales tax does she pay? *(Lesson 10.4)*

    Ⓐ $400   Ⓑ $50

    Ⓒ $40   Ⓓ $8

12. $\overleftrightarrow{AB}$ and $\overleftrightarrow{CD}$ are lines. Find the measure of $\angle a$. *(Lesson 12.1)*

    Ⓐ 180°

    Ⓑ 105°

    Ⓒ 75°

    Ⓓ 57°

Name: _____ **Date:** _____

13. The sides of triangle *ABC* are in whole inches. *AB* = 5 inches and *BC* = 11 inches. Which of these is a possible length for $\overline{AC}$?
(Lesson 13.4)

(A) 3 inches   (B) 6 inches

(C) 12 inches   (D) 16 inches

14. In the trapezoid *PQRS*, $\overline{PS} \parallel \overline{QR}$. Find the measure of *SPR*.
(Lesson 13.5)

(A) 98°

(B) 72°

(C) 52°

(D) 26°

15. Which of these nets can form a triangular pyramid? *(Lesson 14.3)*

(A)

(B)

(C)

(D)

16. How many 1-centimeter cubes can be put into the box? *(Lesson 14.6)*

(A) 38

(B) 1,200

(C) 1,260

(D) 1,620

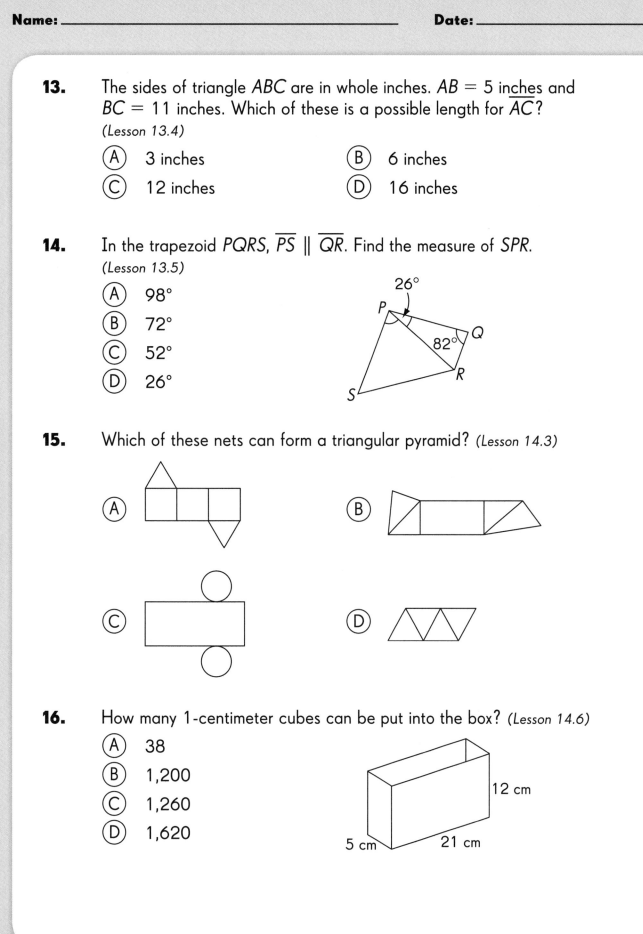

17. What is 0.625 × 400? *(Lesson 2.2)*

 (A) 1000 (B) 250

 (C) 100 (D) 25

18. Find 3.8 × 10³. *(Lesson 2.3)*

 (A) 380 (B) 3,800

 (C) 38,000 (D) 380,000

19. Simplify 30 − {18 − [12 ÷ (20 − 14)]}. *(Lesson 2.7)*

 (A) 14 (B) 10

 (C) 56 (D) 6

20. Which measure is equivalent to 5 kilograms 35 grams? *(Lesson 9.6)*

 (A) 8.5 kilograms

 (B) 5.35 kilograms

 (C) 5.035 kilograms

 (D) 5.00035 kilograms

21. Which of the following is equal to 3,160? *(Lesson 9.3)*

 (A) 3.16 × 10³

 (B) 0.316 × 10³

 (C) 31.6 × 10³

 (D) 316 × 10²

22. What is $12 \div \frac{1}{4}$? *(Lesson 4.6)*

 (A) 3

 (B) $12\frac{1}{4}$

 (C) $11\frac{3}{4}$

 (D) 48

Short Answer

Read the questions carefully. Write your answers in the spaces provided. Show your work.

23. Find the area of the rectangle below. *(Lesson 6.1)*

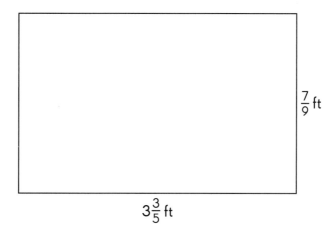

$\frac{7}{9}$ ft

$3\frac{3}{5}$ ft

_____

24. In the figure below, how many more circles must be shaded so that the fraction of shaded circles to the total number of circles is $\frac{2}{3}$? *(Lesson 4.4)*

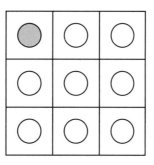

_____

Use the data below for exercises 25 and 26.

Cassia has collected leaves from different plants. She wants to investigate the lengths of the leaves from each plant. She recorded the lengths in the table below.

Length (ft)	$\frac{1}{6}$	$\frac{1}{4}$	$\frac{1}{2}$	$\frac{3}{4}$
Number of Leaves	2	5	7	7

25. Make a line plot to show the data in the table. *(Lesson 11.1)*

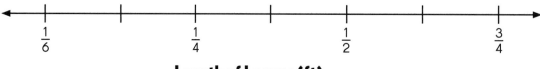

Length of Leaves (ft)

26. Use the data to answer these questions. *(Lesson 11.1)*

a. What is the difference in length between the longest leaf and the shortest leaf?

_____

b. How many more of the long leaves are there than short leaves?

_____

27.   A rectangular tank has a height of 18 centimeters. The area of its base is
225 square centimeters. Find the volume of the tank. *(Lesson 14.6)*

_____

28.   Two pieces of foam are placed in a box to protect the sides of a vase, as
shown in the diagram below. Find the volume of the two pieces of foam.
(Lesson 14.7)

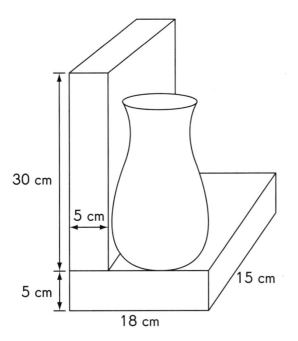

30 cm

5 cm

5 cm

18 cm

15 cm

_____

29. Abe, Belle, and Cathy have a total of $179.50. Abe has $9 more than Belle. Cathy has three times as much as Abe. How much money does Belle have? *(Lesson 9.6)*

_____

30. What is the volume of the solid below, made up of 1-inch cubes? Some of the cubes may be hidden. *(Lesson 14.1)*

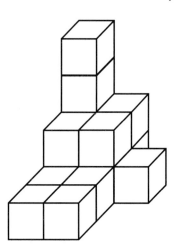

_____

31.   Find the surface area of the triangular prism. *(Lesson 14.4)*

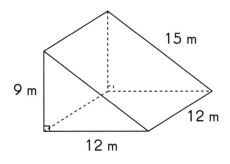

15 m

9 m

12 m

12 m

_____

32.   Use the data in the graph below to answer the questions. The graph
$y = 5x$ shows the cost of different lengths of lumber. *(Lesson 11.3)*

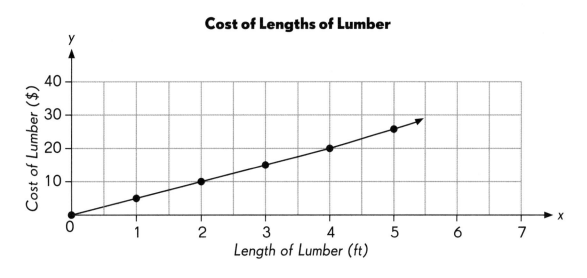

Cost of Lengths of Lumber

Cost of Lumber ($)

Length of Lumber (ft)

a.   What is the cost of a piece of lumber 7 feet long?

_____

b.   What would be the length of a piece of lumber costing $50?

_____

33. The figure below is made up of five identical triangles. The perimeter of the square *ABCD* is 248 inches. Find the area of the whole figure. *(Lesson 6.3)*

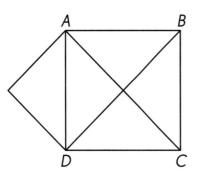

_____

Name: _____ **Date:** _____

34. The ratio of the volume of water in bucket A to the volume of water in bucket B is 3 : 5. The total volume of water in the two buckets is 56 liters. What is the volume of water in bucket B? *(Lesson 7.3)*

_____

35. Write 12 ones and 3 tenths 2 hundredths 5 thousandths in expanded form. *(Lesson 8.1)*

_____

36. What is the value of Δ in the equation? *(Lesson 9.4)*

$9.42 = 9,420 \div \Delta$ _____

37. Order the decimals from least to greatest. *(Lesson 8.2)*
11.05, 11.00, 11.10, 11.009

_____

38. $\frac{3}{8}$ of the regular price of a digital watch is $21. The price of the digital watch after discount is $21. Find the dollar amount of the discount. *(Lesson 10.4)*

_____

Use the data in the bar graph to answer questions 39 and 40.

Favorite Sports of Students

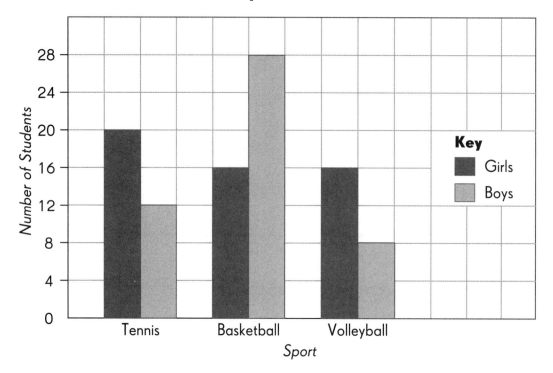

39. For which sport is the difference between the number of boys and girls the greatest? *(Lesson 11.2)*

_____

40. How many more girls than boys prefer tennis? *(Lesson 11.2)*

_____

Use the data in the graph to answer questions 41 and 42.

Conversion Between Gallons and Quarts

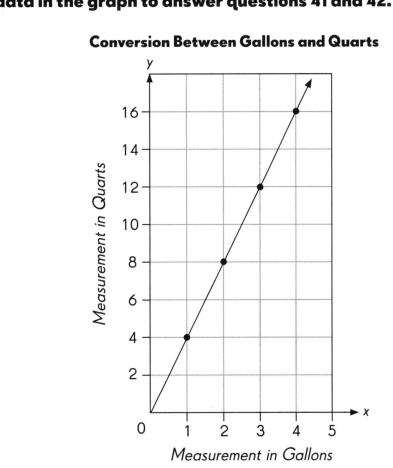

41. Mrs. Richards buys 8 quarts of milk in 4 days. How many gallons of milk does she buy? *(Lesson 11.3)*

_____

42. What is the equation of the graph? *(Lesson 11.3)*

_____

43. Mrs. Mani has 1 orange, 1 apple, 1 peach, and 1 apricot. She has 3 different flavored yogurt bars. She packs one fruit and one yogurt bar into a lunch box. Find the number of combinations she can pack in one box. *(Lesson 11.5)*

_____

44. A box contains 6 red pens, 4 blue pens, 8 green pens, and some black pens. Leslie picks a pen and returns it to the box each time. The outcomes are recorded in the table.

Number of Times a Red Pen is Picked	Number of Times a Blue Pen is Picked	Number of Times a Green Pen is Picked	Number of Times a Black Pen is Picked
8	5	14	3

    a. What is the experimental probability of drawing a green pen? *(Lesson 11.6)*

                             _____

    b. If the theoretical probability of drawing a black pen is $\frac{1}{10}$, how many black pens are in the box? *(Lesson 11.6)*

                             _____

45. $\overleftrightarrow{AB}$, $\overleftrightarrow{CD}$ and $\overleftrightarrow{EF}$ are lines. Find the measures of $\angle x$ and $\angle y$. *(Lessons 12.1 and 12.3)*

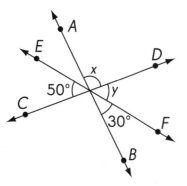

                             m$\angle x =$ _____

                             m$\angle y =$ _____

46.   In triangle *DEF*, *DF* = *EF*. Find the measures of ∠*a* and ∠*b*.
(Lessons 13.2 and 13.3)

m∠*a* = _____

m∠*b* = _____

47.   *ABCD* is a parallelogram and *ADE* is an equilateral triangle. Identify all the angles that have the same measure as ∠*f*. *(Lessons 13.3 and 13.5)*

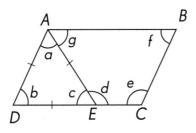

_____

48.   Brian has $50. He buys 10 copies of a book and has *x* dollars left. What is the cost of each book? *(Lesson 5.5)*

_____

49.   How many unit cubes are used to build the solid? *(Lesson 14.1)*

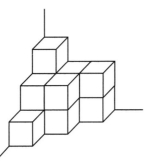

_____

50. *ABCD* is a parallelogram. Find the measure of ∠*DAC*. *(Lesson 13.5)*

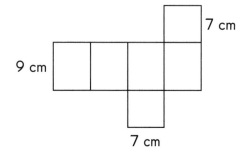

_____

51. The net of a square prism is as given. Use the net to find the surface area of the prism. *(Lesson 14.4)*

_____

52. Express $3\frac{1}{5} + 2\frac{1}{20}$ as a decimal. *(Lesson 3.5)*

_____

53. $\overleftrightarrow{JL}$ is a line. Find the measure of ∠*MKN*. *(Lesson 12.1)*

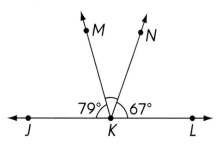

_____

Extended Response
Solve. Show your work.

54. There are 450 seats in a theater. 48% of the seats are occupied.
How many seats are not occupied?

55. The area of a plot of land is 2,496 square meters. A small part
of the land is fenced. The ratio of the total area of the plot of land to
the area that is not fenced is 48 : 31. What is the area of the
land that is not fenced?

56. Harry buys a sofa set that costs $2,000. He pays for it with 12 monthly installments. He also pays 5% interest. What is the total amount he has to pay?

57. Mr. Jacobs buys 20 kilograms of rice at $0.84 per kilogram. He buys 700 grams of shrimp at $1.02 per 100 grams. How much does he spend in total?

58. A fish tank measures 40 centimeters by 25 centimeters by 24 centimeters. It is filled with water from a tap. The fish tank is $\frac{5}{8}$ full in 6 minutes. Find the volume of water that flows from the tap each minute.

59. Mrs. Jackson has $90. She spends $\frac{1}{4}$ of her money on food, $\frac{1}{2}$ of the remainder on clothes and saves the rest. How much does she save?

60. Team A has 42 members. Team B has 18 more members than team A. What percent of the members from team B must be transferred to team A so that team A has as many members as team B?

61. An equal amount of water is poured into two empty tanks, P and Q. Tank P is then $\frac{1}{2}$-filled. What fraction of tank Q is filled with water?

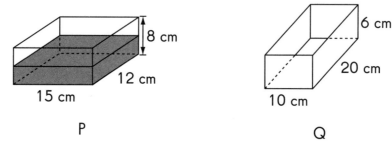

P   Q

62. There is some water in a tank. Water is then poured into the tank until the volume of water is 8 times as much as the initial volume of water in the tank. When another 16.75 liters of water is added, the total volume of water in the tank becomes 20.35 liters. How much water is in the tank at first? Give your answer in liters.

63. Flower pots are placed along a driveway at regular intervals. The distance between two pots is 12 feet.

   a. How long is the driveway if a total of 25 pots, including pots at both ends, are to be placed along it?

   b. If the driveway is 1,080 feet, how many more flower pots are needed?

64. A rectangular tank is half-filled with water. Water is poured into the 10-centimeter cubical tank on the right. How much water is left in the rectangular tank after the cubical tank is filled?

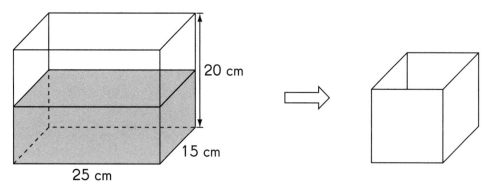

Name: _____ **Date:** _____

Complete the tables and graphs. Then answer the questions.

65. Roy can type 60 words per minute. Annette can type 70 words per minute. Complete the tables below.

Number of Words Typed by Roy

Time (min)	1	2	3	4	5
Number of Words	60				

Number of Words Typed by Annette

Time (min)	1	2	3	4	5
Number of Words	70				

66. Plot the points on a coordinate grid.

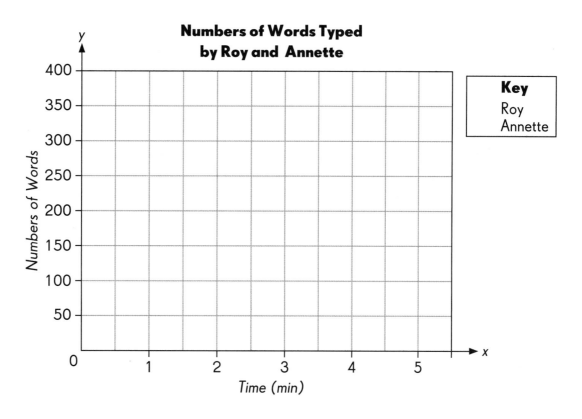

67. How many words do each of them type in 4 minutes?

68. How long does each person take to type 840 words?

69. Estimate the time taken by each person to type 1260 words.

70. Annette typed a document for 15 minutes and then had to leave.
She asked Roy to continue typing from where she had stopped.
Roy took 24 minutes to complete typing the document. How many words were in the document?